HARRISON BLAKEWOOD

The Beginner s Guide to YouTube Success

Everything You Need to Start, Create Engaging Content, and Grow Your Audience

Copyright © 2024 by Harrison Blakewood

All rights reserved. No part of this publication may be reproduced, stored or transmitted in any form or by any means, electronic, mechanical, photocopying, recording, scanning, or otherwise without written permission from the publisher. It is illegal to copy this book, post it to a website, or distribute it by any other means without permission.

First edition

*This book was professionally typeset on Reedsy.
Find out more at reedsy.com*

Contents

1	Introduction	1
2	Chapter 1: Understanding YouTube and Setting Your Goals	3
	Section 1: What is YouTube and Why Start a Channel?	3
	Section 2: Defining Your Purpose and Audience	14
	Section 3: Building a Success-Oriented Mindset	32
3	Chapter 2: Preparing for Your YouTube Journey	52
	Section 1: Setting Up Your YouTube Channel	52
	Section 2: Planning Your Content Strategy	74
	Section 3: Preparing Your Equipment and Tools	93
4	Chapter 3: Creating and Editing Your First Video	114
	Section 1: Writing and Planning Your First Script	114
	Section 2: Shooting Your First Video	131
	Section 3: Editing Like a Pro (Even as a Beginner)	146
5	Chapter 4: Uploading and Sharing Your First Video	164
	Section 1: Uploading Your Video to YouTube	164
	Section 2: Promoting Your First Video	175
	Section 3: Celebrating and Planning Ahead	193
6	Recap and Final Thoughts	209

Recap of the Main Points 209
Final Thoughts and Words of Encouragement 210
7 Ask for a Review 212

1

Introduction

The *Beginner's Guide to YouTube Success* is the ultimate roadmap for anyone eager to dive into the world of YouTube and create a successful channel from the ground up. Whether you're a complete beginner or someone who's ready to take your channel to the next level, this book is designed to help you navigate each step of the journey with ease and confidence.

In the first section, we explore the power of YouTube as a platform, its global reach, and the incredible opportunities it offers for personal and professional growth. We also debunk common myths about starting a channel, showing that you don't need expensive equipment or an expert status to succeed.

Next, we dive into the importance of defining your purpose and understanding your target audience. Setting clear personal and professional goals is essential to success, and we'll guide you through the process of identifying your niche and creating content that resonates with your viewers.

Building a success-oriented mindset is crucial, so we focus on overcoming self-doubt, managing your time effectively, and gaining confidence in front of the camera. These steps will ensure that you remain motivated and focused throughout your YouTube journey.

In the preparation phase, we cover everything you need to know to set up your channel and plan your content strategy. From understanding how to prepare your equipment on a budget to creating a channel design that reflects your brand, we've got you covered.

We also walk you through creating and editing your first video, offering practical tips on scripting, shooting, and editing—even if you're new to the process. By the end, you'll know how to produce high-quality content that captivates your audience.

Finally, we delve into the process of uploading, promoting, and celebrating your first video. We share how to craft attention-grabbing titles, create eye-catching thumbnails, and promote your content to build a loyal following. With these tools, you'll be equipped to share your message with the world and begin your YouTube success story.

This guide offers all the insights you need to make your YouTube dream a reality—step by step, with actionable advice and expert tips for every stage of the journey.

2

Chapter 1: Understanding YouTube and Setting Your Goals

Section 1: What is YouTube and Why Start a Channel?

YouTube's Global Reach

YouTube is not just a platform; it's a global phenomenon. With billions of users worldwide, YouTube offers unparalleled opportunities for creators, brands, and businesses to reach and engage audiences across the globe. In this chapter, we'll explore the vast reach of YouTube, its incredible statistics, and why it's one of the most powerful tools for both personal and professional growth in today's digital world.

1. Overview of YouTube as a Platform

Launched in 2005, YouTube has grown into the world's largest video-sharing platform, revolutionizing the way we consume media and connect with one another. With over **2 billion logged-in monthly users**—and billions of videos watched each day—YouTube is a **powerhouse for content creation and discovery**. It's not just a place to watch funny cat videos or trending challenges; YouTube is where people turn to learn new skills, follow their favorite creators, explore new hobbies, and connect with global communities.

The platform allows users to upload, view, and share videos on virtually any topic imaginable, making it one of the most diverse and accessible platforms for video content. From educational videos to product reviews, vlogs, music, gaming, and beyond, YouTube provides a home for creators of all types, no matter their niche.

What sets YouTube apart is its accessibility. **YouTube is available in over 100 countries** and is localized in more than 80 languages, allowing creators to share their content with a global audience. Whether you're speaking English, Spanish, Mandarin, or any of the other supported languages, your videos have the potential to reach people around the world, making it a truly **international platform**.

The platform is also highly versatile. It offers a range of video formats, including long-form content, live streams, shorts, and community posts, which provide creators with diverse ways to connect with their audience. Whether you're posting a tutorial, hosting a live Q&A, or sharing a short video update, YouTube makes it possible to create content that fits your style.

2. Key Statistics on Audience and Engagement

The statistics surrounding YouTube's audience and engagement are staggering, and they highlight just how powerful the platform can be for anyone looking to build an online presence.

- **2 billion logged-in monthly users**: This means that **almost a third of the internet's population** is active on YouTube, making it an incredibly vast and influential platform.
- **Over 1 billion hours of video watched each day**: YouTube is a hub of continuous activity, with viewers consuming an immense amount of content daily. This offers creators a massive audience to engage with, no matter how niche their content might be.
- **Over 500 hours of video are uploaded to YouTube every minute**: This statistic emphasizes the scale of content creation happening on the platform. The sheer volume of new videos means there's always fresh, exciting content for users to discover.
- **YouTube reaches more 18–34-year-olds and 18–49-year-olds than any TV network in the U.S.**: YouTube has become the go-to platform for younger audiences, and it's now a primary entertainment and educational resource for millions of people worldwide. Its influence has surpassed traditional TV networks, making it an indispensable tool for marketers and creators alike.
- **More than 70% of YouTube views come from mobile devices**: YouTube is primarily a mobile-first platform, meaning that viewers are consuming content on-the-go, whether on smartphones, tablets, or other portable devices.

This accessibility makes YouTube an ideal platform for creators to reach audiences wherever they are.

These statistics demonstrate that YouTube is not only a highly active platform but also an incredibly **engaged one**. Viewers aren't just passively watching—they're actively interacting with content, leaving comments, sharing videos, and subscribing to channels. The level of engagement on YouTube is unparalleled, making it a highly valuable platform for creators looking to build a dedicated and interactive audience.

3. Why YouTube is a Powerful Tool for Personal and Professional Growth

Now that we've explored the vastness of YouTube's reach, let's talk about why this platform is such a powerful tool for **personal and professional growth**.

Personal Growth

For individuals looking to **learn new skills** or expand their knowledge, YouTube is an invaluable resource. Whether you want to learn how to play an instrument, bake a cake, speak a new language, or master a programming language, there's likely a video or series of videos that can help you do just that. YouTube is home to millions of tutorials, guides, and how-tos that can aid in your personal development.

Additionally, YouTube fosters **creativity** by encouraging you to create content, tell your stories, and share your unique perspective. For many, becoming a YouTuber is a journey of self-discovery, helping them build confidence, improve communication skills, and tap into their creative potential. The act of regularly producing content teaches you about perseverance, time management, and the process of refining your craft. It's a platform that encourages continuous learning and improvement, whether you're creating videos or consuming them.

Professional Growth

For professionals, YouTube is a game-changer. It's a fantastic platform for building **personal brands** and positioning yourself as an authority in your field. Whether you're an entrepreneur, educator, consultant, or artist, YouTube offers a way to showcase your expertise, share your knowledge, and connect with potential clients or collaborators. Videos can help establish credibility, promote your services or products, and provide value to your audience, ultimately leading to new opportunities for business growth.

Moreover, YouTube is a powerful tool for **networking and collaboration**. The global nature of the platform allows you to connect with like-minded professionals, brands, and potential partners from around the world. Collaboration can lead to new projects, sponsorships, and partnerships, further propelling your professional success.

And let's not forget about **monetization opportunities**. YouTube offers a variety of ways for creators to generate income, including ads, memberships, sponsorships, and merchandise sales. This ability to monetize content allows creators to turn their passion into a profession, creating a sustainable business model and enabling them to grow their income while doing what they love.

The Benefits of Being a YouTuber

We'll explore the incredible benefits of being a YouTuber. It's not just about creating videos; it's about the opportunities YouTube offers for creativity, community-building, and even generating income. Whether you're considering starting your own channel or already on your way, understanding these key advantages can help you stay motivated and focused as you build your presence on the platform.

1. Opportunities for Creativity and Self-Expression

One of the greatest benefits of being a YouTuber is the **freedom to express yourself creatively**. Unlike other platforms where content is often limited by the format or type of content, YouTube offers virtually unlimited possibilities. Whether you're passionate about cooking, travel, beauty, gaming, education, or even niche hobbies, YouTube allows you to create content that aligns with your personal interests and values.

The beauty of YouTube lies in its diversity of content. You can experiment with different video styles, formats, and editing techniques to find what resonates with both you and your audience. You have complete control over how you present your ideas, your personality, and your passions. There are no rigid rules to follow, and that's where the magic happens. Your creativity can shine through in every video you create, helping you build a unique identity and brand.

This freedom of expression is not only fulfilling but also powerful. As you share your thoughts, experiences, and skills, you're telling a story that is uniquely yours. And the more authentic and true to yourself you are, the more your audience will connect with your content. Being a YouTuber allows you to build a personal brand, turning your hobbies and passions into a platform that the world can access.

2. Potential forBuilding a Community

Another key benefit of being a YouTuber is the ability to **build a community**. The relationships you form with your audience are an integral part of your success on the platform. YouTube is not just a place to share videos; it's a space where people come together to interact, share ideas, and build connections. As your channel grows, you will notice that your viewers are no longer just passive consumers of content—they become an active part of your creative journey.

Building a community on YouTube is not just about gaining subscribers; it's about creating a space where people feel they belong. Your audience will engage with your content, leave comments, share their own experiences, and even form friendships with one another. This sense of belonging can be incredibly rewarding, both for you and your viewers. The relationships you cultivate with your audience can lead to deeper connections, collaborations, and a sense of shared purpose.

Furthermore, YouTube offers a variety of tools to help you engage with your community, such as live streams, community posts, and comment sections. These features allow you to interact with your audience in real-time, answer questions, and even create content based on their feedback. Over time, you'll develop a loyal following—people who trust your voice, appreciate your content, and feel connected to your brand.

3. Income Generation Possibilities through Monetization

While many people start YouTube as a creative outlet, one of the most appealing aspects of the platform is its **potential for income generation**. Although monetizing your channel doesn't happen overnight, YouTube provides several ways to turn your passion into profit. The best part? The opportunities are available to creators of all sizes.

The most well-known method of monetization is through the **YouTube Partner Program**. Once you meet the eligibility requirements, you can start earning money from ads placed on your videos. But that's just the beginning. YouTube also offers other monetization options, such as **Super Chats** during live streams, **Channel Memberships** for exclusive content, and **YouTube Premium revenue**, which provides additional income from viewers who subscribe to YouTube's ad-free service.

But the income potential doesn't stop with ads. Many YouTubers also earn money through **sponsorships** and **affiliate marketing**. Brands are always looking for creators to promote their products, and if your content aligns with their target audience, you can build lucrative partnerships. Affiliate marketing is another great way to earn money by promoting products or services in your videos and earning a commission on any sales generated through your unique links.

In addition, YouTube offers creators the chance to sell **merchandise** directly to their audience through integrations with platforms like Teespring or Spreadshop. Fans who love your content can support you by purchasing branded merchandise, creating another revenue stream. The possibilities for income generation are vast, and the more you grow your channel and audience, the more these opportunities will expand.

Common Myths About Starting a YouTube Channel

When it comes to starting a YouTube channel, there are plenty of misconceptions that can hold potential creators back from diving in. Whether it's worrying about the costs, feeling like you need to be an expert, or doubting that there's still room for new creators, these myths can create unnecessary barriers. In this chapter, we'll tackle the three most common myths about YouTube, debunking them with the truth and giving you the confidence to start your own channel.

1. "You Need Expensive Equipment to Start."

One of the most widespread myths about starting a YouTube channel is the idea that you need to invest in expensive equipment to create professional-quality content. The truth is, you don't need the latest camera, high-end microphones, or fancy lighting setups to get started on YouTube. While these tools can certainly enhance your content, **they're not a requirement for success**.

In fact, many successful YouTubers began with nothing more than a smartphone or a basic webcam. The key to making great content is **creativity and consistency**, not the price tag of your equipment. With modern smartphones, you can record high-quality video and audio. You can even edit your videos using free or low-cost software available online.

If you're concerned about lighting, consider natural light or affordable ring lights that can make a world of difference without breaking the bank. And as for audio? A simple lapel mic can drastically improve the sound quality over your phone's built-in microphone, and these don't cost much at all.

Remember, your content's value lies in your message, your creativity, and how you engage with your audience. As you grow, you can reinvest in better equipment, but don't let the fear of expensive gear stop you from starting.

2. *"You Need to Be an Expert to Succeed."*

Another myth that keeps many aspiring YouTubers from launching their channels is the belief that you need to be an expert in a particular field to succeed. **This couldn't be further from the truth.** In fact, YouTube is home to a wide variety of creators, ranging from experts in their fields to those simply sharing their passion and journey along the way.

While expertise can certainly help, what matters most is **authenticity** and **passion**. Many successful YouTubers start by simply sharing what they're learning or experimenting with—whether it's cooking, fitness, DIY projects, or even trying out new hobbies. Your audience doesn't need you to be an expert; they need you to be **genuine** and **relatable**. People connect with creators who are transparent about their experiences and share their personal stories, struggles, and growth.

If you're passionate about something and willing to learn as you go, your audience will follow you for your journey—not just your final destination. As you grow and gain more experience, you'll naturally become more knowledgeable, and that will be reflected in your content. But don't wait to become an "expert" before starting—your journey is just as valuable as the destination.

3. "It's Too Late to Start a YouTube Channel."

This myth is perhaps the most discouraging for new creators: the belief that it's too late to start a YouTube channel because the platform is already saturated with content. The reality is that **there's always room for fresh voices, unique perspectives, and new content**.

YouTube is a massive platform with billions of users, and it's constantly evolving. While it's true that there are many creators on YouTube, **the demand for content is just as vast**. People are always looking for something new, whether it's a fresh take on a popular trend, a niche topic, or a unique approach to storytelling.

Think of it this way: no two people are the same, and no two creators will ever bring the exact same perspective. The success of a YouTube channel doesn't rely on how long the platform has been around or how many videos are already out there; it relies on your ability to connect with your audience, offer value, and stay consistent.

In fact, YouTube's algorithm is designed to promote diverse content, and there's always an audience for what you have to offer. It's not about competing with the biggest creators—it's about finding your unique voice and carving out your own space. So, don't worry about the "competition." If you're passionate and consistent, there's always room for your voice on YouTube.

Why Start a YouTube Channel Now?

Despite its massive popularity, YouTube continues to grow, offering endless opportunities for new creators. With its free-to-use model, user-friendly interface, and robust analytics tools, YouTube empowers anyone to share their voice and build an audience.

Whether you want to share your expertise, grow a business, or pursue a creative hobby, YouTube provides the tools and audience to turn your ideas into reality.

Section 2: Defining Your Purpose and Audience

What Do You Want to Achieve?

Before you start creating videos, uploading content, or planning your channel, it's essential to take a step back and think about what you actually want to achieve. YouTube can be an incredibly powerful tool for both **personal** and **professional growth**, but to make the most of it, you need to know where you're headed. In this chapter, we'll explore how to identify your goals, align your YouTube channel with your long-term objectives, and set **measurable, achievable goals** that will guide you on your journey.

1. Identifying Personal and Professional Goals

The first step in your YouTube journey is understanding why you're starting a channel in the first place. What do you want to achieve personally and professionally by being a creator on YouTube? Answering these questions will help you set the foundation for your channel's direction.

Personal Goals

Personal goals are about what you want to accomplish for yourself, both in terms of growth and fulfillment. Think about the following:

- **Learning and Development**: Do you want to improve your skills in video editing, storytelling, or speaking in front of the camera? YouTube can be an excellent tool for self-improvement. If you've always wanted to enhance your public speaking, for example, creating videos can help you become more confident and comfortable in front of an audience.
- **Creative Expression**: Are you looking to express your creativity and share your passions with the world? Perhaps you want to use YouTube to showcase your artistic skills, try new hobbies, or tell stories. Your personal goal might be centered on creating content that excites and inspires you.
- **Building Confidence**: Starting a YouTube channel can help you break out of your comfort zone. If you've always been shy or uncertain about putting yourself out there, YouTube can be a way to build confidence and learn how to communicate effectively with an audience.
- **Personal Fulfillment**: Sometimes, personal goals are as simple as sharing what you know with others and having fun in the process. You might just want to create videos that are meaningful to you, whether for enjoyment or to leave a legacy of some kind.

Professional Goals

Your professional goals are often tied to your career or business ambitions. YouTube has the potential to become a powerful tool for professional growth, so identifying clear professional goals can help you leverage the platform for career advancement or business success. Consider the following:

- **Building a Personal Brand**: Do you want to establish yourself as an expert in a specific field? YouTube can help you build your authority, especially if you share valuable content in your area of expertise. Whether you're a consultant, coach, educator, or entrepreneur, YouTube can be an incredible platform for growing your personal brand and reputation.
- **Monetizing Your Content**: Are you looking to turn your YouTube channel into a source of income? Many creators make money from YouTube through ads, sponsorships, merchandise sales, and more. Monetizing your channel might be one of your key professional goals, and understanding how to do this effectively is essential.
- **Networking and Collaboration**: YouTube is also a great place to collaborate with others in your field. Building relationships with other creators or industry professionals can open doors for collaborations, partnerships, and new business opportunities. If you're looking to connect with like-minded people, YouTube could serve as the ideal platform for this.
- **Driving Traffic to a Business**: If you own a business or have a side hustle, YouTube can be a fantastic way to attract customers, clients, or followers. By creating content that

showcases your products, services, or expertise, you can drive traffic to your website, increase sales, and build a loyal customer base.

2. Aligning YouTube with Long-Term Objectives

Once you've identified your personal and professional goals, it's important to align your YouTube efforts with your **long-term objectives**. Your channel should serve as a stepping stone toward achieving the bigger picture, not just a short-term project. This alignment will help you stay focused, even when the going gets tough.

Creating a Vision for Your Channel

Think about where you want to be in the next few years and how YouTube fits into that vision. For instance, if your long-term objective is to become a thought leader in your industry, your YouTube content should focus on providing value to your target audience and establishing your credibility. If your goal is to launch a business, your YouTube content could center around promoting your products and services while building an audience that is interested in what you offer.

Ask yourself these questions:

- Where do I see myself in 3 to 5 years?
- How can YouTube help me get there?
- What type of content do I need to create to stay aligned with my long-term vision?

By keeping your broader objectives in mind, you can ensure

that your YouTube strategy supports those goals rather than deviating from them. It's important to remember that **YouTube success doesn't happen overnight**, and having a long-term vision will help you stay focused during times when you're not seeing immediate results.

Consistency with Purpose

Your YouTube content should reflect your long-term purpose. Whether it's educational, entertaining, or promotional, every video you create should contribute to the overall narrative you want to tell about yourself or your brand. Consistency in your content style, messaging, and values will help you build a coherent online presence that is aligned with your goals.

3. Setting Measurable, Achievable Goals

Once you've identified your personal and professional goals and aligned them with your long-term objectives, the next step is to break those goals down into **measurable and achievable** steps. This is where you can turn your dreams into actionable tasks that will keep you on track toward success.

Creating SMART Goals

A helpful framework for setting goals is the **SMART method**, which stands for **Specific, Measurable, Achievable, Relevant, and Time-bound**. By using this approach, you can ensure that your goals are clear, realistic, and focused.

- **Specific**: Your goal should be clear and well-defined.

Instead of saying, "I want to grow my channel," say, "I want to gain 500 subscribers in the next 3 months by posting weekly videos about cooking tutorials."
- **Measurable**: Set goals that can be tracked. For example, "I want to get 100 new subscribers every month" is a measurable goal. This helps you gauge progress and stay motivated.
- **Achievable**: Your goals should be realistic and within your reach. Setting goals that are too ambitious can lead to frustration, while setting goals that are too easy can hinder your growth. Be honest with yourself about what you can accomplish in a given timeframe.
- **Relevant**: Ensure that your goals align with your overall personal and professional aspirations. For instance, if you're building a business, your goal might be to create videos that showcase your product's features and benefits.
- **Time-bound**: Every goal should have a deadline. Setting a timeline for achieving your goals creates a sense of urgency and helps you stay focused. For example, "I will upload 4 videos per month for the next 6 months."

Tracking Your Progress

As you set and work toward your goals, make sure to **track your progress** regularly. This can be done through YouTube's built-in analytics tools, which provide data on metrics like views, watch time, and audience engagement. Tracking allows you to adjust your strategy as needed and celebrate small wins along the way.

Finding Your Niche

When starting a YouTube channel, one of the most important decisions you'll make is **finding your niche**. Your niche defines your unique space on the platform, where you can carve out a dedicated audience and create content that resonates with them. But with billions of videos already online, how do you figure out what you should focus on? In this chapter, we'll guide you through the process of finding your niche by exploring what topics excite you, researching popular and underserved niches, and aligning your niche with your skills and interests.

1. What Topics Excite You?

The first and most crucial step in finding your niche is to reflect on your **passions** and **interests**. You're going to spend a lot of time creating content around your chosen niche, so it's essential that the topics you select genuinely excite and motivate you. This will make the content creation process enjoyable and sustainable over the long term.

Passion Drives Consistency

When you're passionate about something, it's easier to stay consistent with creating content. The YouTube algorithm favors consistent uploads, and your audience will appreciate your regular contributions. If you're creating content around a topic that you genuinely care about, the effort won't feel like a chore—it will feel rewarding.

Start by asking yourself some introspective questions:

- **What are you passionate about?** What do you find

yourself talking about to friends or family without prompting? Maybe it's something related to hobbies like gaming, cooking, fitness, or art.
- **What do you love learning about?** If there's a subject you find yourself constantly diving into—whether it's through books, articles, or podcasts—this could be an indication that it's a topic worth exploring on YouTube.
- **What hobbies or skills have you developed over time?** You don't have to be an expert to start a channel, but having some background in a particular area can give you a strong foundation. Whether it's photography, DIY projects, or knitting, if it excites you, it could be your niche.

The key is to pick a topic that keeps you engaged and excited over time. You're more likely to stay committed to the channel and create content that feels authentic if the subject matter is something that you love. Passion also naturally connects with audiences who share similar interests.

2. Researching Popular and Underserved Niches

Once you have a general idea of topics that excite you, it's time to **research the broader landscape** of YouTube and see how your interests align with current trends and demand. This step will help you identify niches that are both **popular** and **underserved**, which can give you a competitive advantage.

Understanding Popular Niches

Popular niches are those that attract large audiences. These niches typically have a lot of content already, and while they present opportunities, they can also be **highly competitive**. Examples include:

- **Beauty and fashion**
- **Fitness and wellness**
- **Gaming**
- **Travel and vlogging**
- **Technology and gadgets**
- **Cooking and food**

These niches have tons of content, but they also come with established audiences looking for fresh perspectives. If you're considering one of these popular niches, think about how you can **offer something unique** to stand out in a crowded space. It could be your personal experience, your specific approach, or your sense of humor. Your unique perspective is key to distinguishing yourself from others in these saturated spaces.

Finding Underserved Niches

While popular niches are valuable, it can be equally rewarding to explore **underserved niches**—topics that have **potential demand** but haven't been fully explored or saturated with content yet. These niches tend to have less competition, which can make it easier for new creators to gain visibility. They also allow for **innovation and growth**.

To find these underserved niches, consider:

- **Google Trends**: Use Google Trends to discover rising topics. It's a great way to gauge whether a topic is gaining interest and could benefit from more content.
- **YouTube Search Bar**: Use YouTube's search feature to see what suggestions come up when you type in terms related to your interests. This can give you a sense of what people are searching for but not finding enough content about.
- **Social Media and Forums**: Platforms like Reddit, Twitter, and niche Facebook groups are excellent for spotting conversations that aren't getting enough attention on YouTube yet. Join relevant groups or communities and observe what people are discussing or looking for. You might uncover a topic that has untapped potential.

Remember, there's no need to be afraid of **niches that seem too small**. A smaller audience can still be incredibly **engaged and loyal**, and serving them well can help you grow your channel more quickly than competing in an overcrowded niche.

3. Aligning Your Niche with Your Skills and Interests

Now that you have an idea of what topics excite you and have done some research on the popularity and potential of different niches, the next step is to **align your niche with your skills and expertise**.

Leverage Your Strengths

Your niche should be something that plays to your **strengths and skills**. If you're naturally good at something or have gained experience through personal practice, that can be a solid foundation for your channel.

For example:

- **Do you have a background in photography or videography?** Maybe a channel on **photography tips** or **video production** could be your niche.
- **Are you an expert in a specific language or culture?** This could open doors for a channel that focuses on **language learning** or **cultural exploration**.
- **Do you have a knack for DIY projects?** Your channel could provide **step-by-step tutorials** for crafting, home improvement, or woodworking.

If you don't yet feel like an expert, that's perfectly fine. Many successful YouTubers have started by sharing their learning journey or documenting how they **improve their skills over time**. For example, if you're into fitness but are still learning about health and nutrition, you could create a channel where you share your experiences, progress, and challenges—this creates a relatable and authentic connection with viewers who are on the same path.

Matching Skills with Passion

While it's essential to choose a niche you're excited about, it's also important to choose one where you can bring something of **value**. Do you have the skills to create high-quality content in your niche? For example, if you're passionate about cooking but aren't confident in your ability to create appealing food videos, consider developing those skills through practice and research before committing to that niche.

Alternatively, if you're great at speaking on camera or explaining concepts clearly, you might consider educational or tutorial-style content, even if you're just starting out. There's an audience for creators who are **learning alongside them**, especially in niches that focus on self-improvement.

Understanding Your Target Audience

To create successful YouTube content, it's essential to understand **who your audience is** and **what they need**. Your audience is the heart of your YouTube channel, and catering to their needs and preferences is key to building a loyal community and growing your channel. In this chapter, we'll explore how to identify your target audience, use tools to research audience demographics, and create content that truly resonates with the people you want to reach.

1. Who Are They, and What Are Their Needs?

Understanding your target audience starts with identifying who they are and what they're looking for. This is more than just demographic information; it's about understanding their

interests, behaviors, and pain points.

Demographics: Age, Gender, Location

Start by defining basic demographic information:

- **Age**: Are you targeting teenagers, young adults, middle-aged viewers, or seniors? Different age groups have different preferences in terms of content type, language, and tone.
- **Gender**: Consider if your content appeals more to a specific gender or is gender-neutral. This will help shape your messaging, tone, and even aesthetic.
- **Location**: Are you focusing on a global audience, or is your content specific to a particular region or country? Understanding where your audience is located can help you customize your content for local interests, cultural references, and language preferences.

However, **demographics are only part of the picture**. To truly understand your audience, you need to dig deeper into their **psychographics**—what motivates them, their challenges, and how they engage with content.

Psychographics: Interests, Problems, and Desires

Your audience's **interests** and **problems** are often the driving forces behind why they come to YouTube. Ask yourself questions like:

- **What are their goals or challenges?** For example, if your

channel is about fitness, your audience might be looking for ways to lose weight, build muscle, or improve their overall health.
- **What questions do they have?** Think about the kind of questions people ask related to your niche. Are they looking for tutorials, tips, entertainment, or educational content? Understanding these questions can help you create videos that provide direct answers.
- **What emotions are they experiencing?** Emotions play a significant role in content engagement. Are your viewers looking for motivation, relaxation, excitement, or inspiration? If you can tap into these emotional needs, your content will feel more relatable.

By aligning your content with what your audience **wants and needs**, you'll make your channel more relevant and impactful. You'll create a **stronger connection** and be seen as a **valuable resource**.

2. Tools for Researching Audience Demographics

Once you have a general sense of your target audience, it's important to **validate your assumptions** and get more detailed data. YouTube offers several tools and resources to help you **research your audience's demographics**, interests, and behaviors.

YouTube Analytics

The best place to start is **YouTube Analytics**, a powerful tool that offers a wealth of data about your viewers. Once you've uploaded a few videos, you can dive into:

- **Age and gender breakdown**: You can see the age range and gender of your viewers, which will help you better understand the type of content they might enjoy.
- **Geography**: YouTube Analytics shows you where your viewers are located, which can inform decisions about language, regional references, and content relevance.
- **Watch time and engagement**: This tells you how long people are watching your videos and whether they're interacting with your content (likes, comments, shares). It can give you insights into what kind of content resonates most with your audience.

Google Analytics

If you have a **website** or blog that complements your YouTube channel, **Google Analytics** can offer additional insights into your audience's demographics, behavior, and interests. For example, you can see what people are searching for before they come to your site, what pages they spend time on, and how long they stay.

Social Media Insights

Don't forget about the insights you can gather from **social media platforms** like Instagram, Twitter, or Facebook. These platforms offer demographic data on your followers, including age, location, and interests. By comparing your social media audience to your YouTube viewers, you can identify trends and make sure you're targeting the right group.

Audience Surveys and Feedback

A simple yet effective way to get to know your audience is by asking them directly. Consider using surveys or polls on YouTube (via the Community tab), Instagram Stories, or email lists. Ask questions like:

- What content would you like to see more of?
- What are your biggest struggles related to the topic I cover?
- How do you consume content on YouTube—do you prefer long-form videos or short clips?

This feedback will not only help you understand your audience better but also **show them that you care** about their needs and opinions.

3. How to Create Content That Resonates

Once you've gathered data about who your audience is and what they need, the next step is to **create content that resonates** with them. Here's how you can ensure your videos meet their expectations and offer real value:

Solve Problems or Answer Questions

At the core of successful content is the ability to **solve problems** or **answer questions** that your audience has. Think about what your viewers are struggling with and create videos that offer solutions. For example:

- If your target audience is beginners in photography, create content like "5 Easy Photography Tips for Beginners."
- If your audience is interested in personal finance, you could make videos like "How to Budget Effectively for Young Adults."

Make sure that your content is **actionable**, providing real takeaways that viewers can apply in their lives. The more you can **empower your audience** through your content, the more they'll trust you as a valuable resource.

Tailor Content to Your Audience's Preferences

Once you have demographic and psychographic data, you can tailor your content to fit their preferences. For example:

- If your audience is younger and enjoys quick, high-energy content, focus on short-form videos or fast-paced editing.
- If your audience is older and enjoys in-depth tutorials, focus on long-form, detailed videos with a more relaxed pace.
- If your audience enjoys humor, make sure your videos have a fun and lighthearted tone.

Remember that **content style** matters. Your videos should not only provide the right information but also be **engaging** and **entertaining**. The presentation of your content, including tone, visuals, and editing, should align with your audience's expectations.

Be Authentic and Relatable

One of the key factors in building a loyal following is being **authentic**. Audiences connect with creators who are genuine and transparent. Share your personal experiences, struggles, and successes. Being vulnerable or showing your true personality can help create a **deeper connection** with your viewers.

For example, if you're giving fitness advice, don't just focus on perfect results. Share your fitness journey, including the challenges you face, the mistakes you make, and how you overcome them. This authenticity will make your content more relatable and your audience more loyal.

Encourage Engagement

Finally, don't forget to encourage your audience to **engage with your content**. Ask them to like, comment, and subscribe, but also ask for their feedback and input. Questions like "What are some tips you would add to this list?" or "What topics would you like to see covered next?" can generate interaction and help you understand your audience even better.

The more engaged your audience is, the more likely they are to share your videos and recommend them to others. **Building a community** around your content can significantly increase your channel's reach and success.

Section 3: Building a Success-Oriented Mindset

Overcoming Self-Doubt

Starting something new—especially something as public and potentially vulnerable as a YouTube channel—can stir up a lot of **self-doubt**. Whether it's fear of failure, the pressure to be perfect, or simply the fear of being judged, these emotions can hold you back from taking the leap. But **self-doubt** doesn't have to stop you from pursuing your YouTube journey. In this chapter, we'll explore how to **recognize** and **address** these fears, embrace **imperfection** as part of the creative process, and learn to **celebrate small wins** along the way. By the end, you'll be equipped with the mindset to push through fear and build a successful channel with confidence.

1. Recognizing and Addressing Fears About Starting

The first step in overcoming self-doubt is **recognizing** that the fears you're feeling are completely normal. Most new YouTubers experience some level of fear or anxiety before they hit "record" for the first time. It's part of the human experience, especially when venturing into something unfamiliar.

Common Fears You Might Encounter:

- **Fear of judgment**: "What will people think of me? Will they criticize me?"
- **Fear of failure**: "What if my videos don't get any views or engagement?"

- **Imposter syndrome**: "I'm not an expert—who am I to create content on this topic?"
- **Fear of technology**: "What if I mess up the editing, sound, or video quality?"

These fears can be paralyzing, but it's important to acknowledge them and address them head-on.

Addressing the Fear of Judgment

One of the biggest fears that holds people back from starting is the fear of being judged. We live in a world where everyone has an opinion, and the thought of putting yourself and your work out there for **public scrutiny** can be intimidating. However, it's important to remember that **everyone starts somewhere**. Every successful YouTuber had their **first video**—and it wasn't perfect.

Rather than focusing on the potential for criticism, **shift your focus to your audience's needs**. Think about the value you're providing. What knowledge, entertainment, or experience do you bring to the table? If your content helps even one person or entertains them, that's a win. Don't get bogged down by the fear of judgment; instead, **embrace the idea that everyone has their unique voice** to contribute.

Conquering the Fear of Failure

Another common fear is the fear of failure. "What if my videos don't get any views?" is a question that many new creators ask. The reality is that **failure is part of the process**. It's through failure and mistakes that we learn and improve.

No one becomes a successful YouTuber overnight. The most important thing is to **keep going** and learn from your experiences.

Take a moment to reframe failure: rather than viewing it as something to avoid, see it as **feedback**. If a video doesn't perform well, don't take it personally. Instead, analyze it—what could you improve? Were your titles and thumbnails eye-catching enough? Did the content resonate with your audience? Use this information to improve and try again.

Overcoming Imposter Syndrome

Imposter syndrome, the feeling that you're not qualified to create content or that you don't know enough, can be incredibly limiting. But the truth is, **you don't need to be an expert to start**. Many successful YouTubers began by documenting their journey or sharing what they were learning. People are often more interested in **your perspective** than in your credentials.

Remember, **everyone is learning**. The process of growth and discovery is what makes your journey relatable. **Share your learning process**, ask questions, and engage with your audience—your authenticity will resonate far more than trying to be perfect. The key is to **be yourself** and let your genuine enthusiasm for the subject shine through.

2. Embracing Imperfection as Part of the Process

One of the biggest traps creators fall into is the idea that they need to be perfect from day one. This belief can paralyze you from even starting. However, **imperfection is a natural part**

of growth—and it's essential to embrace it. The best content is often authentic, raw, and unpolished. The process of creation should be fun and experimental, not rigid and stressful.

Why Imperfection is Essential

- **Growth comes from practice**: The more you create, the better you'll get. Each video you make is an opportunity to improve your skills, whether it's with editing, scripting, or presentation. Perfection is unattainable in the beginning; it's all about **progress over perfection**.
- **Your audience will connect with you**: Imperfection can make you more relatable. If your videos are polished but stiff, they may feel less authentic. But if you're okay with showing your **human side**, even if it means making mistakes on camera, your audience will appreciate your vulnerability and see you as more approachable.
- **Perfectionism stifles creativity**: If you're constantly aiming for perfection, you may be holding yourself back from trying new things. Creativity thrives in an environment where you're willing to take risks and make mistakes. Don't be afraid to experiment with new ideas, formats, or approaches.

Instead of striving for perfection, focus on **improving over time**. Set realistic expectations for yourself and celebrate the little wins along the way.

How to Let Go of Perfectionism

- **Give yourself permission to fail**: Understand that **failure is temporary**. Mistakes are part of learning and growing.
- **Keep your first videos simple**: Don't worry about having the best editing, camera, or lighting. Start with what you have, and focus on delivering value. The more you practice, the better your production quality will get.
- **Be kind to yourself**: Treat yourself with the same understanding and patience that you would extend to a friend who is learning something new.

3. Celebrating Small Wins Along the Way

In the journey of building a YouTube channel, it can be easy to get caught up in the big picture—like reaching a certain number of subscribers or going viral. While those goals are important, it's equally essential to celebrate the **small wins** that happen along the way. These moments, no matter how small, are a reflection of your progress.

What Counts as a Small Win?

- **Your first comment**: It might not be thousands of comments, but your first thoughtful comment from a viewer is a big deal. It means someone saw your video, engaged with it, and cared enough to leave feedback.
- **Your first 100 views**: Hitting your first milestone of views might seem small, but it represents the beginning of building your audience.

- **Getting your first subscriber**: Each new subscriber means someone believes in your content enough to want more of it.
- **Improving your content**: If you notice your videos getting more polished or your confidence growing in front of the camera, that's a huge win!
- **Positive feedback**: Whether it's someone saying they learned something from your video or simply enjoying it, this type of feedback is invaluable and should be celebrated.

Why Small Wins Matter

Small wins can keep you motivated and remind you that **you're making progress**, even if the big results take time. Celebrating these moments will help you maintain momentum and **keep you going through the difficult times**. It's easy to get discouraged when success doesn't come quickly, but by focusing on what you've already achieved, you'll build a sense of **pride** and **satisfaction** in the process.

How to Celebrate Small Wins

- **Acknowledge your progress**: Take a moment to reflect on what you've achieved. Look back at your first video, and compare it to your recent ones. Celebrate how far you've come!
- **Share your achievements**: Share your small wins with your audience or close friends. People love to celebrate alongside you, and it reinforces your sense of accomplishment.

- **Reward yourself**: Treat yourself to something special when you hit a milestone. It could be a small indulgence like your favorite snack or a break to recharge.

Time Management for Beginners

Starting and maintaining a YouTube channel is an exciting venture, but like any other commitment, it requires effective **time management**. For many creators, YouTube is just one part of a busy life. Whether you're balancing a full-time job, school, family responsibilities, or other personal commitments, managing your time effectively is essential for success. In this chapter, we'll explore how to **balance YouTube with other responsibilities**, **set aside dedicated time** for planning and creating, and how to use **tools and apps** to stay organized so you can stay on top of your content creation.

1. Balancing YouTube with Other Responsibilities

One of the biggest challenges when starting a YouTube channel, especially for beginners, is **balancing content creation with other aspects of life**. Many creators begin their channels while still juggling full-time jobs, school, or personal responsibilities. Finding a balance is key to avoiding burnout and staying productive.

Assessing Your Current Schedule

The first step in managing your time effectively is to **assess how you currently spend your day**. Look at your current commitments and determine where you might be able to fit YouTube work into your routine. This might involve:

- **Evaluating your work, school, or family schedule**: Identify your busiest times and potential pockets of free time.
- **Understanding your energy levels**: Are you most productive in the mornings or late at night? Knowing your peak productivity hours will help you plan your YouTube tasks effectively.

Prioritizing Your Responsibilities

You might find that YouTube is just one of many important things in your life. It's important to **prioritize** your responsibilities:

- **Set boundaries**: Be clear about when and how long you can devote to YouTube tasks each week. This ensures that YouTube doesn't negatively impact other areas of your life.
- **Create realistic goals**: Understand that you don't need to create content every day, especially in the beginning. Even dedicating a couple of hours each week can be enough to start building momentum.

Time-Blocking for Efficiency

Time-blocking is a great technique to balance multiple responsibilities. This involves dedicating specific blocks of time during the day for different tasks or activities. For example:

- Block out an hour on your weekends for planning your next video.
- Schedule specific days during the week for shooting or editing.
- Set aside 15-minute intervals each day for engaging with your community or responding to comments.

By blocking time on your calendar for YouTube, you'll be able to **avoid distractions** and remain focused during these designated work periods.

Delegating or Outsourcing Tasks

As your channel grows, consider delegating or outsourcing tasks that take up a significant amount of time. For instance, if editing videos is time-consuming, you can hire a freelance editor. This allows you to focus more on content creation and growing your audience. If outsourcing isn't an option right away, **find ways to streamline** processes, like using templates or pre-built workflows, to save time on repetitive tasks.

2. Setting Aside Dedicated Time for Planning and Creating

The next step in managing your time effectively as a YouTuber is to **set aside dedicated time** for **planning and content creation**. This is where you organize your ideas, write scripts, shoot your videos, and edit them. Having a specific time set aside for these tasks will help ensure that you make consistent progress on your channel.

Time for Planning Your Content

Effective planning is the key to a successful YouTube channel. Without a clear roadmap, it's easy to get overwhelmed or lose motivation. Set aside dedicated time for:

- **Brainstorming video ideas**: Set a specific time each week or month to brainstorm new video ideas. This can be as simple as a 30-minute session where you jot down every idea that comes to mind. Over time, you'll develop a content pool to choose from when it's time to film.
- **Content calendars**: A content calendar is a great tool to plan and schedule your videos in advance. This allows you to visualize when each video will go live and helps you avoid last-minute scrambling. Block off specific dates for planning content, researching, and writing scripts, so you stay on track.

Time for Filming and Editing

Once your videos are planned out, **dedicate time** for the actual filming and editing process. For filming:

- **Set a regular shooting schedule**: Whether it's once a week or once a month, having a consistent filming routine ensures that your content creation process remains steady. Try to set up a shooting environment where you can easily film, such as a dedicated space with good lighting.
- **Keep filming sessions efficient**: If you're shooting multiple videos in one go, try batching your content. This means filming several videos in one session so you don't have to constantly set up your gear.

When it comes to editing:

- **Schedule time for editing**: Editing can take a significant amount of time, especially for beginners. It's important to allocate sufficient time for this task, whether it's an hour a day or a couple of sessions per week.
- **Use editing templates**: To speed up the editing process, use editing templates for things like intros, outros, and transitions. This can save you a lot of time in the long run.

Creating Time Buffers

While scheduling is crucial, it's also important to leave yourself **some buffer time.** Life can be unpredictable, and tasks may take longer than expected. Having extra time built into your schedule ensures that you don't feel rushed, stressed, or overwhelmed by deadlines.

3. Tools and Apps for Staying Organized

Staying organized is critical for efficient time management, especially when you're juggling multiple responsibilities. Fortunately, there are several tools and apps available to help you stay on track, plan your content, and streamline your workflows.

Project Management Tools

Project management apps help you organize your tasks, set deadlines, and track progress. Some of the best tools include:

- **Trello**: Trello uses boards and cards to help you visually organize tasks. You can create a board for your YouTube channel, with cards for individual videos, and add deadlines, checklists, and labels to stay organized.
- **Asana**: Asana is another popular project management tool that allows you to create projects, assign tasks, and set deadlines. It's perfect for tracking your video creation process from start to finish.
- **Notion**: Notion is a versatile tool that can be used for project management, note-taking, and content planning. It allows you to create databases, calendars, and to-do lists, all in one place.

Content Planning Tools

For planning your content and organizing ideas, consider using these tools:

- **Google Calendar**: Set up reminders for filming, editing, and uploading. Google Calendar can help you visualize your content schedule and make sure you stay on track.
- **Evernote**: Evernote is an excellent tool for organizing research, brainstorming ideas, and keeping track of notes for each video. You can create notebooks for different topics, store scripts, and clip useful articles.
- **CoSchedule**: This tool is designed for content creators, allowing you to plan, schedule, and publish your posts across multiple platforms, including YouTube. It's perfect for those who want to streamline their content marketing and distribution.

Time-Tracking Apps

To make sure you're staying on track with your time management, consider using time-tracking apps like:

- **Toggl**: Toggl helps you track how much time you're spending on different tasks. You can log the time spent on filming, editing, and other YouTube-related activities, giving you a clear picture of where your time is going.
- **RescueTime**: RescueTime runs in the background on your computer or phone and tracks your activity. It can give you insights into how much time you're spending on productive tasks versus distractions.

Task Automation

If you find yourself spending a lot of time on repetitive tasks, automation tools can save you time:

- **Zapier**: Zapier connects your favorite apps and automates tasks between them. For instance, you can set up a workflow that automatically posts your new YouTube video on Twitter or Facebook.
- **IFTTT**: Similar to Zapier, IFTTT allows you to create automation recipes that link different apps and services together, streamlining your workflow.

Building Confidence On-Camera

One of the biggest hurdles for new YouTubers is the fear of being on camera. Whether it's the fear of making mistakes, the worry about how you look or sound, or the anxiety of speaking in front of an audience, **building confidence on-camera** is essential for creating engaging and authentic content. In this chapter, we'll explore practical strategies to help you **overcome camera shyness**, **enhance your presentation skills**, and start creating practice videos that will make you feel more comfortable and confident in front of the camera.

1. Practicing Speaking to the Camera

The key to building confidence on camera is **practice**. Just like any new skill, the more you practice, the better you'll become, and the more natural you'll feel. Speaking directly to the camera can feel awkward at first, but with time, it will become second nature.

Start Small and Simple

Don't put too much pressure on yourself in the beginning. Start by speaking to the camera in low-stakes situations:

- **Record short introductions**: Begin by recording a 30-second introduction where you simply say your name and what your channel is about. This can be a quick, simple exercise to get comfortable with speaking to the camera without feeling overwhelmed.
- **Use a mirror**: Before hitting record, speak in front of a mirror. This helps you become more aware of your body language and facial expressions, making it easier to translate that naturalness onto the camera.

Speak Slowly and Clearly

When speaking to the camera, especially if you're nervous, it's easy to rush your words. However, speaking too quickly can make your message harder to understand and can add to your anxiety. Instead:

- **Pause regularly**: Take short pauses between sentences to give yourself time to breathe and think. This will also make your speech sound more deliberate and confident.
- **Focus on clarity**: Try to enunciate your words clearly. Practice speaking slowly to avoid stumbling over your words, and take time to think before you speak. This will

make your videos sound more professional.

Practice with Different Angles

To get comfortable with being on camera, experiment with **different camera angles**:

- **Face the camera head-on**: This is the most natural angle and will help you feel more connected with your audience.
- **Side angles**: Occasionally switching to side angles or slightly different camera positions will help you get used to how you appear from different perspectives, helping you become less self-conscious about your appearance.

Don't Worry About Perfection

It's natural to feel self-conscious when you're recording yourself. However, don't expect perfection. The first few times you speak to the camera, you might feel stiff or awkward, and that's okay. **Embrace the imperfections**. **Every take** doesn't need to be flawless—what matters is consistency and improvement over time.

2. Techniques for Improving Presentation Skills

While practicing speaking to the camera is important, **presentation skills** are just as crucial for building confidence and delivering content that engages your audience. Whether you're recording a tutorial, an opinion piece, or a vlog, having good presentation skills will ensure that your audience stays engaged with your content.

Posture and Body Language

Good posture and body language are critical when presenting on camera:

- **Stand or sit up straight**: This makes you appear more confident and professional. Avoid slouching or leaning back too much in your chair, as this can make you seem less engaged with your audience.
- **Use gestures**: Hand gestures can help emphasize points and make you appear more enthusiastic. Just be sure not to overdo it—subtle gestures that match the tone of your voice are the most effective.
- **Maintain eye contact**: Looking directly at the camera lens gives the impression that you're speaking directly to your viewers, which fosters a sense of connection and trust. If you're reading from a script or notes, occasionally look back at the camera to break the monotony.

Voice Control and Tone

Your voice plays a huge role in how your presentation is received:

- **Vary your tone**: A monotone voice can sound flat and disengaging. Practice varying your tone to match the emotions you want to convey. For example, increase your volume slightly when you're excited, or slow down when you want to emphasize a key point.
- **Pace yourself**: A confident speaker doesn't rush. Practice speaking slowly and deliberately, especially when explain-

ing complicated concepts. Pausing after important points can give your audience time to absorb the information.
- **Project your voice**: Speak with authority and confidence. Even if you're nervous, projecting your voice ensures that you come across as more assertive and credible.

Engage Your Audience

The best YouTubers don't just speak at their audience—they engage with them. Try these techniques to make your videos feel more interactive:

- **Ask questions**: Incorporate questions into your videos to encourage viewers to think and interact with you. For example, "What do you think about this? Let me know in the comments!"
- **Use personal stories**: Sharing personal anecdotes can help make your content more relatable. It will also make you feel less robotic and more authentic.
- **Smile**: A genuine smile can make you appear more approachable and confident. It also helps you feel more comfortable on camera.

Prepare with a Script or Bullet Points

If you're nervous about losing track of what you want to say, use a script or bullet points to guide your presentation. Writing down your ideas beforehand can help you organize your thoughts and reduce the pressure of speaking off the cuff. Over time, you'll feel more comfortable improvising and delivering more spontaneous content, but using a script or outline is a great tool for beginners.

3. Creating Your First Practice Videos

Now that you've practiced speaking to the camera and have learned some basic presentation techniques, it's time to put everything together and start creating your **first practice videos**. Don't worry about perfection—this is all about **building your confidence** and learning by doing.

Start with Low-Stakes Videos

Begin with videos that don't require high production value or heavy editing. This will take the pressure off and allow you to focus solely on improving your on-camera presence. Some practice video ideas include:

- **Introduction video**: Introduce yourself and talk about why you started your YouTube channel. This simple video can help you get comfortable speaking directly to the camera.
- **Practice Q&A**: Answer a few simple questions about yourself or your channel. This format allows you to practice thinking on your feet while keeping the conversation natural.
- **Reaction or commentary video**: Watch a video or share an opinion on a trending topic and film your reaction. This type of video allows you to be more expressive and practice your tone and body language.

Film Short Clips

If you're feeling nervous, start by recording shorter clips. There's no need to film long videos at first—aim for 2-5 minutes of content to keep it manageable. You can always build up to longer videos as you gain confidence.

Watch and Reflect

After filming your practice videos, take the time to **watch them**. While it might feel awkward at first, this is an excellent opportunity to evaluate how you appear on camera. Pay attention to your:

- **Tone of voice**: Are you speaking clearly and with energy?
- **Body language**: Are you engaging with the camera? Are you using gestures naturally?
- **Confidence**: Does it look like you're having fun? Are you smiling and relaxed?

Don't be overly critical of yourself. Instead, focus on what went well and what you can improve on for next time.

Keep Practicing

The more practice you get, the better you'll become. Don't be discouraged if your first videos don't feel perfect—remember, it's all about progress, not perfection. Keep filming practice videos and gradually increase the complexity of your content as you grow more comfortable

3

Chapter 2: Preparing for Your YouTube Journey

Before diving into the production of videos, it's essential to set the groundwork for a successful YouTube channel. This chapter will guide you through setting up your YouTube account, designing your branding, and planning your content strategy. We'll also cover how to choose the right equipment and tools to get started without overwhelming your budget.

Section 1: Setting Up Your YouTube Channel

Your YouTube channel is your digital storefront. It's where viewers will discover your content and get a sense of who you are. Creating and optimizing your channel correctly is the first step in building a successful YouTube presence.

Creating a YouTube Account

Creating a YouTube account is the first step toward becoming a content creator on the platform. Whether you want to create a personal channel, a professional one, or a brand-based channel, YouTube offers a straightforward process to get started. In this chapter, we'll walk you through the step-by-step guide to creating your YouTube account, how to choose the right name for your channel, and how to verify your account and enable essential features to set yourself up for success.

1. Step-by-Step Guide to Creating an Account

Before you can upload videos, interact with your audience, or customize your channel, you need to create a YouTube account. Here's how to get started:

Step 1: Create a Google Account

YouTube is owned by Google, so in order to create a YouTube account, you must first have a Google account. If you already have a Google account (for Gmail or other Google services), you can use that to sign in to YouTube. If you don't have one, follow these steps:

- **Go to Google's Account Creation page**: Open your web browser and go to Google's sign-up page.
- **Fill in the required information**: Enter your first and last name, email address, and a password for your new account. You'll also need to confirm your password to ensure it's correct.
- **Agree to Google's terms and conditions**: Read through the terms, then click "I Agree" to continue with the account creation process.

Once your Google account is set up, you're ready to move on to creating your YouTube channel!

Step 2: Sign In to YouTube

- Open your web browser and go to YouTube.
- Click on the "Sign In" button in the upper-right corner of the screen. (see fig. 1)
- Enter your newly created Google account details (email and password) and click "Next."

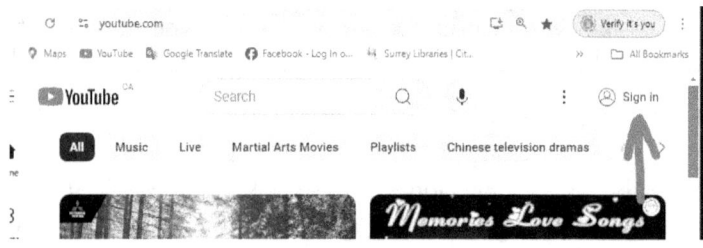

fig. 1

You're now signed in to YouTube, but you still need to create your channel.

Step 3: Create Your YouTube Channel

- Once signed in, click on your profile icon in the upper-right corner of the screen.
- Select "Your Channel" from the drop-down menu.
- You'll be prompted to create your channel. Click on **"Create Channel."** (see fig. 2)

- YouTube will ask you to create a name for your channel. If you're using your Google account name, it will appear automatically, but you can change it to something else.

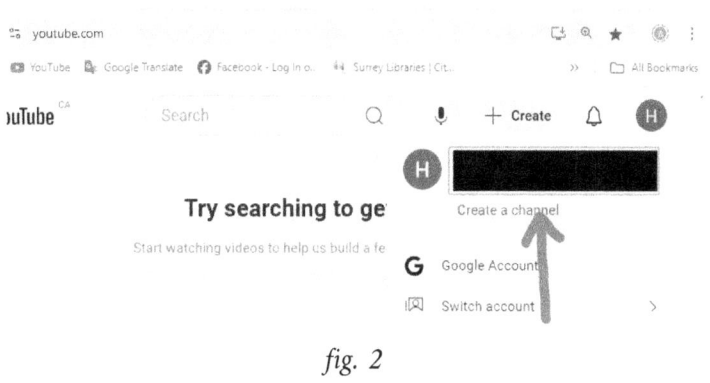

fig. 2

That's it! Your YouTube channel is now created, and you're ready to start customizing it.

2. Choosing the Right Name for Your Channel

The name of your YouTube channel is one of the most important aspects of your brand identity. It should be catchy, memorable, and relevant to the content you plan to create. Here's how to choose the right name:

Consider Your Content

Think about the content you will be creating and the audience you want to attract. Your channel name should give people a clear idea of what they can expect. For example:

- If you plan on making beauty tutorials, consider something related to makeup or beauty.
- If you're creating tech reviews, your name could reflect technology or gadgets.

Keep It Short and Memorable

Short and simple names are easier for viewers to remember and find. Avoid using long, complicated words or phrases that might be hard to spell or pronounce.

Make It Unique

Do some research to ensure your chosen name isn't already taken. A unique name makes it easier for your channel to stand out and ensures there's no confusion with other channels. You can check if your name is available by simply typing it into the YouTube search bar.

Brand Consistency

If you already have social media accounts (like Instagram, Twitter, or Facebook), try to keep your YouTube name consistent with your other profiles. This will make it easier for people to find you across different platforms.

Consider Future Growth

While it's important to choose a name that reflects your current content, also think about the future. Will your channel's content evolve over time? Choose a name that's flexible enough to grow with you.

Examples of Great Channel Names:

- **Tech Talk with Tom** – Clear and specific to tech content.
- **Simply Fitness** – Focuses on fitness and health.
- **The Daily Read** – Suitable for a book review or reading channel.
- **Travel Vibes** – A good name for a travel vlog.

3. Verifying Your Account and Enabling Features

Now that you've created your YouTube channel, there are a few additional steps you'll need to take to unlock extra features that can enhance your experience as a creator.

Step 1: Verifying Your YouTube Account

Verifying your YouTube account is crucial for unlocking important features such as uploading longer videos (over 15 minutes), live streaming, and using custom thumbnails. Here's how to do it:

- **Go to YouTube Studio**: On your YouTube homepage, click on your profile icon in the upper-right corner and select **YouTube Studio**. (see fig. 3)

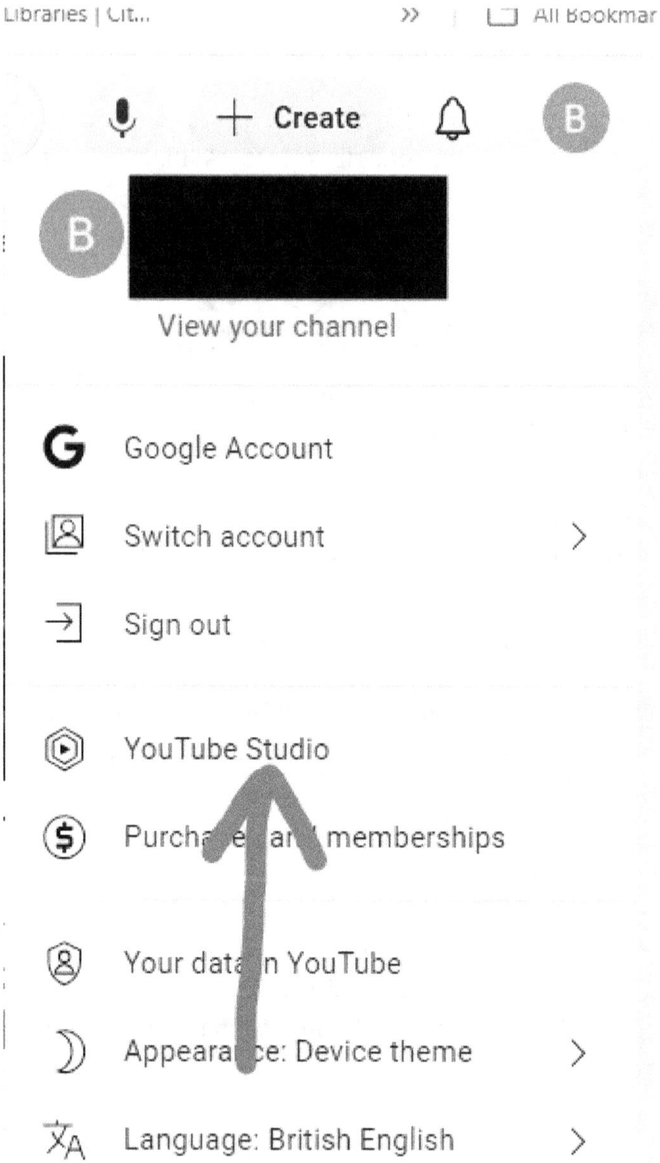

THE BEGINNER S GUIDE TO YOUTUBE SUCCESS

Libraries | Cit...   »   All Bookmar

🎤   **+ Create**   🔔   B

B

View your channel

G   Google Account

👤   Switch account   >

→   Sign out

◉   YouTube Studio

$ Purchases and memberships

👤   Your data in YouTube

☾   Appearance: Device theme   >

🗛   Language: British English   >

fig. 3

- **Access Verification Settings**: In the left-hand menu, click on **Settings** at the bottom (see fig. 4). Under the "Channel" tab, select **Feature Eligibility**. (see fig. 5)

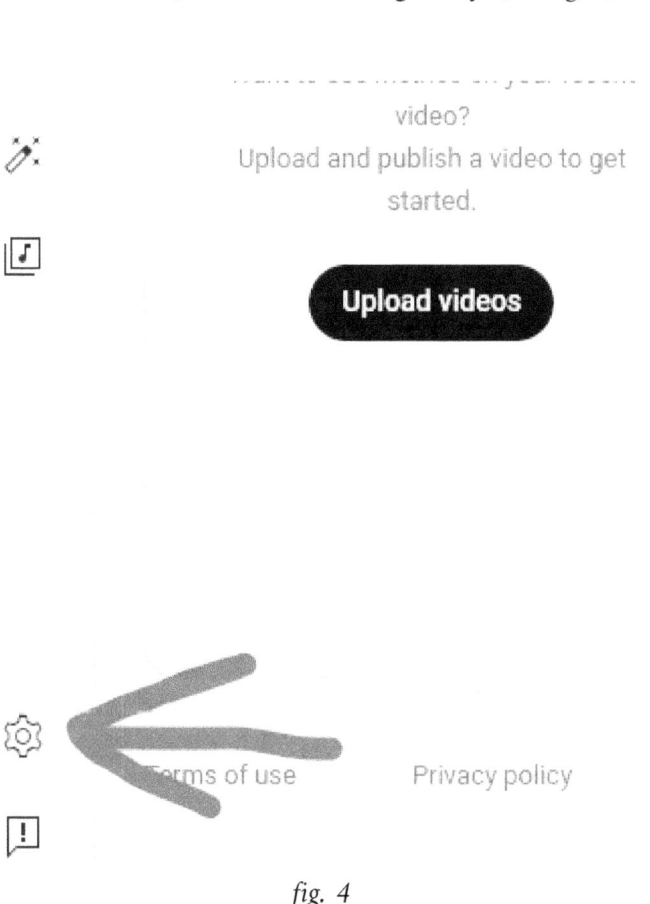

fig. 4

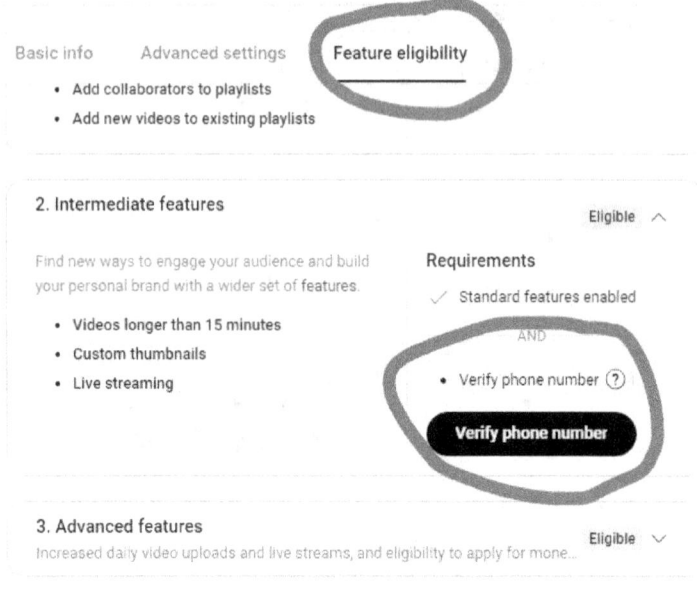

fig. 5

- **Verify your account**: You'll see an option to verify your account. YouTube will ask you to **enter your phone number** (see fig.5). This is to confirm that you're not a bot. You'll receive a text message with a verification code. Enter the code, and you'll be verified!

Step 2: Enabling Custom Thumbnails

Custom thumbnails help make your videos more clickable and appealing. Once your account is verified, you can enable custom thumbnails:

- **Go to YouTube Studio**: Click on your profile icon and select **YouTube Studio**.
- **Upload a Video**: Click on the "Upload Video" button, and during the upload process, you'll have the option to upload a **custom thumbnail**.
- **Designing a Thumbnail**: Make sure your thumbnail is visually appealing, represents your video's content accurately, and includes bold text or images that attract attention.

Step 3: Enabling Live Streaming

Once your account is verified, you can also enable live streaming. Live streaming is a great way to engage with your audience in real-time. To enable live streaming:

- **Go to YouTube Studio** and click on the **"Create"** button (camera icon) in the top-right corner.
- Select **"Go Live"** to access the live streaming feature.
- YouTube may require you to wait 24 hours before your first live stream, so plan ahead.

Step 4: Setting Up Monetization (Optional)

Once your channel grows and you're eligible for monetization, you'll want to set up AdSense to earn money from ads placed on your videos. To set this up:

- **Go to YouTube Studio** and click on **Monetization** under the "Channel" tab.
- Follow the instructions to connect your YouTube channel

with Google AdSense. You'll need to meet YouTube's eligibility requirements for monetization, including having at least 1,000 subscribers and 4,000 watch hours.

·

Designing Your Channel Branding

Your YouTube channel branding is one of the most important elements in building a recognizable and professional online presence. Strong branding helps you stand out in a crowded platform, build trust with your audience, and convey the essence of your content. In this chapter, we will explore how to design your channel branding, covering the creation of a **compelling channel description**, the design of an **eye-catching channel banner** and **logo**, and how to **establish a consistent theme and style** for your channel.

1. Crafting a Compelling Channel Description

Your **channel description** is the first place potential subscribers will look to understand what your content is about and why they should subscribe. It's your opportunity to sell your channel in a few short sentences, so it's essential that it reflects your personality and goals clearly.

Write a Clear and Concise Overview

Begin by telling your audience exactly what your channel is about. Think of it as a "mission statement" for your channel:

- **What is the purpose of your channel?** Are you sharing

educational content, tutorials, reviews, vlogs, or something else?
- **Who is your target audience?** Be specific about who will benefit from your content.
- **Why should people subscribe?** Highlight what makes your channel unique. Is it your perspective, your expertise, or your personality?

Example:

"Welcome to The Daily Read, where book lovers come together to discover exciting new reads, join in-depth discussions, and share reviews. Whether you're into fiction, nonfiction, or graphic novels, our reviews and recommendations will help you find your next great read!"

Incorporate Keywords for Discoverability

To help your channel get found, incorporate **keywords** that your target audience may be searching for. These should be related to your niche and content. For example, if your channel is about cooking, you might include words like "easy recipes," "healthy cooking," or "meal prep."

"Here at *Healthy Bites*, we create delicious and nutritious meals for busy people who want to eat healthy on a budget. From quick weeknight dinners to meal prep tips, we're here to make healthy eating easy!"

Add a Personal Touch

Your description should reflect your voice and personality. Write as though you're speaking directly to your audience. Let them know why you're passionate about the content you create and what they can expect from your videos. A little personal flair can go a long way in building a connection with viewers.

Include a Call to Action

Encourage people to take action after reading your description. This could be something as simple as subscribing to your channel or following you on social media for updates.

Example Call to Action:
"Subscribe today and join our community of book lovers for weekly reviews and recommendations!"

2. Creating an Eye-Catching Channel Banner and Logo

Your **channel banner** and **logo** are the first visual elements people see when they visit your channel. These images should reflect your content and branding and help make a strong first impression.

Designing Your Channel Banner

Your channel banner (also known as your channel art) is the large image that appears at the top of your YouTube channel page. It's an important part of your branding because it's the first thing people see when they visit your channel. Here's how to create a banner that works:

- **Size and Dimensions**: The recommended size for your YouTube banner is **2560 x 1440 pixels** with a maximum file size of **6 MB**. Be sure to keep important elements in the **center safe area** (1546 x 423 pixels) so they don't get cut off on different screen sizes.
- **Brand Colors and Fonts**: Use colors that reflect your personality and the mood of your content. Consistency is key. Choose fonts that are readable and professional. Make sure the fonts align with your style and the type of content you create. For example, a cooking channel might use warm, inviting colors, while a tech channel might opt for sleek, modern tones.
- **Images and Graphics**: Use high-quality images or graphics that reflect your content. If your channel focuses on food, a clean image of a beautifully prepared dish can work wonders. If it's a travel vlog, a stunning landscape or travel shots can give visitors a taste of your adventures.
- **Consistency**: Make sure your banner matches the tone and theme of your videos. If you have an educational channel, your banner should convey professionalism; if your channel is about humor or entertainment, make it fun and lighthearted.

Tools for Designing Your Banner:

- **Canva**: A user-friendly online tool with free templates for YouTube banners.
- **Adobe Spark**: A versatile design tool for creating custom banners and other graphics.
- **Fotor**: Another easy-to-use platform with banner templates.

Designing Your Channel Logo

Your logo should be simple, memorable, and scalable. A great logo helps create a professional image and makes it easier for people to recognize your channel. Here's how to create one:

- **Simplicity**: Keep it clean and simple. You don't need to overcomplicate your logo with too many details. A logo should be recognizable even at small sizes.
- **Relevance**: Make sure your logo aligns with your channel's content. For example, a fitness channel might incorporate weights, a yoga mat, or a body silhouette, while a travel channel might use a globe or a plane.
- **Scalability**: Your logo should look good at different sizes, from being displayed on your channel to appearing as a small icon on mobile devices.
- **Color Choice**: Stick to a color palette that aligns with your branding. Don't use too many colors—usually, one or two strong colors are enough.

Example:

A simple logo for a beauty channel might be a stylized lipstick or brush, with a minimalist font for the channel name.

Tools for Designing Your Logo:

- **Canva**: Offers templates and customizable elements for creating a logo.
- **Logo Maker**: A tool that helps you design logos for free with easy-to-use templates.
- **Hatchful by Shopify**: Another free online logo design tool with options for various industries.

3. Establishing a Consistent Theme and Style

Consistency in your channel branding is crucial for building a strong and recognizable identity. A consistent theme will make your channel look professional and help viewers connect with your content.

Create a Color Scheme

Choose a consistent color scheme that will be used across all of your branding elements—your channel banner, logo, thumbnails, and any other visual content. Consistent colors make your brand recognizable and visually appealing.

- Pick two or three main colors that reflect your content and personality. For example, a health and wellness channel might use green and blue for a fresh and calming effect.
- Avoid using too many colors that can overwhelm your viewers or make your branding look inconsistent.

Consistency in Thumbnails

Your **thumbnails** are an extension of your channel branding. They appear in search results, suggested videos, and playlists, so it's essential that they're visually consistent and align with your overall theme.

- Use the same color scheme and fonts in your thumbnails.
- Incorporate similar design elements (such as borders, icons, or logos) in each thumbnail to make them easily recognizable as your content.

Create a Channel Trailer

Your **channel trailer** (see fig. 6) is another opportunity to establish a consistent theme. This video should introduce new visitors to your content, your style, and what they can expect from your videos. Ensure the tone of the trailer matches your channel's branding—whether it's casual, energetic, or professional.

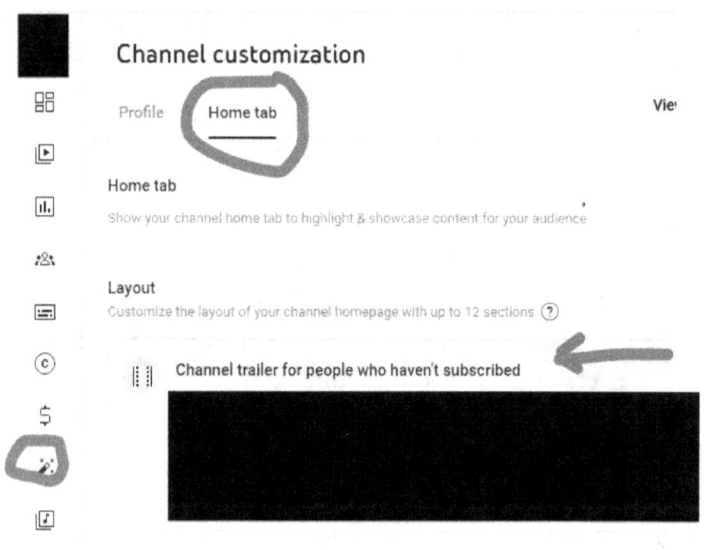

fig. 6

Optimizing Your Channel for Success

To succeed on YouTube, it's not enough to just upload great videos—you also need to optimize your channel to make it discoverable, organized, and connected to your other platforms. Optimization is a crucial step in ensuring that your content reaches the right audience and that your channel is set up to grow. In this chapter, we'll explore how to optimize your YouTube channel for success by focusing on **keywords and tags**, **adding social media and website links**, and **organizing your content with playlists**.

1. Importance of Channel Keywords and Tags

When it comes to YouTube, searchability is key to reaching new viewers. One of the best ways to make your content discoverable is by using **keywords** and **tags** that align with what your audience is searching for. These tools will help YouTube's algorithm understand your content and recommend it to the right people.

Channel Keywords

Channel keywords are words or phrases that describe your content as a whole and tell YouTube what your channel is about. These keywords will help your channel show up in search results when people are looking for content similar to yours.

Here's how to add channel keywords:

- **Go to YouTube Studio**: Sign into YouTube and click on your profile icon in the upper-right corner. Select **YouTube Studio**.

- **Open Settings**: On the left side of the screen, click **Settings** at the bottom.
- **Select Channel**: In the settings menu, click on **Channel**, and then go to the **Basic Info** tab.
- **Add Your Keywords**: In the "Channel Keywords" section, you can enter relevant keywords. Think about what your potential audience might search for. For example, if you're a tech reviewer, keywords might include "tech reviews," "gadgets," "smartphones," and "electronics."

Tips for choosing keywords:

- Think about **search intent**. What would someone type if they were looking for your content?
- Use tools like **Google Trends**, **Keyword Planner**, or **VidIQ** to find popular search terms in your niche.

Tags for Individual Videos

While channel keywords are for your overall content, **tags** are specific to each video. Tags help YouTube understand what your video is about and which searches it should appear for. Here's how to add tags to your videos:

- **Go to YouTube Studio**: Upload your video, then click on the **Video Details** tab.
- **Add Tags**: In the "Tags" section, enter words and phrases that describe your video's content. Use a combination of broad and specific tags. For example, for a video on "How to Set Up a Home Studio," you might use tags like "home studio setup," "recording studio tips," and "how to start a

YouTube channel."

Tagging Tips:

- Use **long-tail keywords**—phrases that are more specific but less competitive (e.g., "best beginner tech gadgets" instead of just "tech gadgets").
- Include **variations** of your main keywords to capture different search terms.

By strategically using channel keywords and video tags, you increase your chances of being discovered by a broader audience.

2. Adding Links to Social Media and Websites

Your YouTube channel should not exist in a vacuum. To truly build your brand, you need to connect your YouTube presence with your other platforms and make it easy for viewers to engage with you outside of YouTube.

Add Social Media Links to Your Channel

YouTube allows you to add links to your social media profiles, websites, or other platforms. This provides a seamless way for viewers to follow you elsewhere, building a stronger relationship and increasing your reach. Here's how to do it:

- **Go to YouTube Studio**: Sign into YouTube and click on **YouTube Studio** from the drop-down menu.
- **Open Customization**: In the left-hand menu, click on

Customization, then go to the **Basic Info** tab.
- **Add Links**: Scroll down to the "Links" section, where you can add up to five links. You can include links to your **Instagram, Twitter, TikTok, personal website, email**, or other relevant pages.
- **Display Links on Your Channel**: These links will appear on the top of your channel homepage. You can choose whether you want them to appear as icons or full URLs.

Tips for Adding Links:

- Make sure the links are relevant to your audience. If you're a fashion vlogger, links to your online store, Instagram, or brand collaborations would be ideal.
- Add a **call to action** in your video descriptions or channel banner, encouraging viewers to check out your other platforms.

Include Links in Your Video Descriptions

Every video description gives you an opportunity to share more links. Whether it's to your social media, affiliate products, or a blog, make sure to add valuable links to each description:

Example: "Follow me on Instagram for behind-the-scenes content: [Instagram handle]. Check out my blog for more tips: [Blog link]."

Adding links to your social media accounts and website helps you grow your following across platforms and makes it easy for people to connect with you.

3. Setting Up Playlists for Content Organization

Playlists are a powerful tool on YouTube, both for organizing your content and improving the viewing experience for your audience. Playlists help YouTube's algorithm understand your content and can even increase watch time by automatically playing related videos.

Why Playlists Matter

- **Content Organization**: Playlists allow you to group similar videos together, making it easier for viewers to find content they're interested in. For example, if you have a cooking channel, you might create playlists like "Quick Weeknight Dinners," "Healthy Meal Prep," and "Desserts."
- **Increased Watch Time**: When videos in a playlist automatically play one after another, viewers are more likely to watch multiple videos in one session, which improves your overall watch time.
- **Better Discovery**: Playlists are indexed by YouTube and can show up in search results, making it easier for viewers to find your content in groups.

How to Set Up Playlists

- **Create a Playlist**: Go to **YouTube Studio**, click on **Playlists** in the left menu, and click the **New Playlist** button. Enter a title and a description for the playlist. Make it clear what kind of content the playlist contains.
- **Add Videos to Playlists**: You can add videos to a playlist as you upload them, or go to an existing playlist and click

Add Videos. You can also choose to automatically add new videos to a playlist based on certain rules.
- **Organize Your Playlist**: Arrange your playlist videos in a logical order—whether that's in a specific sequence or by category (e.g., "Beginner Tips" first, followed by more advanced tutorials).

Tips for Playlists:

- **Descriptive Titles**: Use clear, descriptive titles for your playlists to help viewers understand what they can expect to watch.
- **Optimized Descriptions**: Include relevant keywords in your playlist descriptions to help with discoverability.
- **Consistent Playlist Themes**: Create playlists that align with your channel's themes (e.g., educational videos, product reviews, vlogs) so viewers know what type of content they'll find.

Section 2: Planning Your Content Strategy

A strong content strategy is vital for consistent growth on YouTube. This section will help you brainstorm ideas, plan your first video series, and organize a content calendar.

Choosing Content Ideas

Choosing the right content ideas is one of the most critical steps to building a successful YouTube channel. Your content needs to resonate with your audience, stay true to your niche, and align with the goals of your channel. In this chapter, we'll walk through the process of brainstorming content ideas, leveraging tools like **Google Trends** and **TubeBuddy**, and validating your ideas through **audience research**. By the end of this chapter, you'll have a clear framework for coming up with content ideas that will help you grow your channel and keep your viewers engaged.

1. Brainstorming Topics Based on Your Niche

The first step in choosing content ideas is to understand your niche thoroughly. Whether your channel is about beauty, tech, gaming, education, or cooking, your content must be aligned with the interests of your audience and your area of expertise.

Start with Your Passion

Think about the things you're most passionate about within your niche. What are the topics that excite you, make you want to dive deeper, or that you're curious to explore? When you create content that aligns with your interests, it will come across more authentically, and you're more likely to stay motivated in the long run.

Examples:

- **Tech Channel**: If you love gadgets, you might brainstorm ideas like "Top 5 Budget Smartphones," "Unboxing New Tech," or "Tech News and Updates."
- **Cooking Channel**: If you're passionate about healthy

eating, your content ideas might include "Quick and Easy Vegan Recipes" or "How to Meal Prep for a Week."

Explore Subtopics Within Your Niche

Once you have a general sense of your niche, narrow it down to specific **subtopics**. This allows you to create more focused content and attract a specific audience. Breaking your niche down into smaller, more targeted areas will also help keep your content fresh and give you more ideas to explore.

For example, if you have a **travel** channel:

- You could break your content into **destinations** (e.g., "Best Places to Visit in Europe"), **travel tips** (e.g., "Packing Hacks for Solo Travelers"), or **budget travel** (e.g., "How to Travel on a Budget in Asia").

Analyze Your Competitors

Look at what other creators in your niche are doing. You can learn a lot from seeing what works for others—without copying their ideas. Identify gaps or areas where you can bring your unique perspective. Maybe other channels are doing similar content, but you could approach it with a fresh angle.

Tips for brainstorming:

- Keep a list of content ideas in a notebook or digital document as they come to you. This will help you avoid running out of ideas later on.
- Look for **seasonal** content opportunities, like holiday-themed videos or events, which can give you a boost of

relevant ideas.

2. Using Tools Like Google Trends and TubeBuddy

Once you have a few content ideas in mind, it's important to validate their potential. Are people actually searching for these topics? This is where tools like **Google Trends** and **TubeBuddy** come in handy. These tools will help you evaluate the popularity of topics and refine your ideas to better fit your audience's interests.

Using Google Trends

Google Trends allows you to see how popular specific search terms are over time. You can use it to gauge whether your content idea is trending or gaining interest.

Here's how to use Google Trends:

- **Search for Topics**: Enter your topic or keyword into Google Trends. For example, if you're thinking of making a video about "smartphone reviews," type that into the search bar.
- **Analyze Trends**: Google Trends will show you how the search volume for that topic has changed over time. Is it increasing in popularity, or is it a passing trend? Look for long-term growth rather than short spikes.
- **Compare Topics**: You can compare multiple search terms to see which one is more popular. For example, compare "smartphone reviews" to "laptop reviews" to see which topic might have a bigger potential audience.
- **Check Regional Interest**: If you want to target a specific

region, Google Trends also allows you to see where your chosen topics are most popular. This can help you tailor your content to the interests of people in specific countries or cities.

Google Trends Tip: You can filter results by **category** (e.g., tech, education, etc.) and by **time range** to get more specific data. This will help you spot relevant content ideas with high potential.

Using TubeBuddy

TubeBuddy is a YouTube-certified tool that provides insights directly from the YouTube platform. TubeBuddy offers a range of tools designed to help creators optimize their content, from keyword research to video SEO.

Here's how TubeBuddy can help:

- **Keyword Explorer**: Use the Keyword Explorer to find **popular search terms** related to your content idea. TubeBuddy will show you the search volume, competition, and overall "score" for each keyword, helping you pick the best keywords for your video.
- **Related Searches**: TubeBuddy also shows you **related search terms** and long-tail keywords that people are searching for. This can help you discover content angles you may not have thought of.
- **Tag Suggestions**: TubeBuddy can suggest tags for your video that will help it rank higher in search results. Using the right tags makes it easier for your videos to show up in YouTube search, which can increase your views.

- **Competitor Research**: TubeBuddy allows you to spy on your competitors, helping you identify what topics they're covering and which ones are getting the most traction.

By using tools like Google Trends and TubeBuddy, you can make more informed decisions about which topics are worth pursuing.

3. Validating Ideas Through Audience Research

Once you've narrowed down your content ideas, it's time to validate them by understanding your audience's needs. Creating content that resonates with your audience is key to building a loyal following and increasing engagement.

Poll Your Audience

Use **YouTube polls**, **community posts**, or **Instagram stories** to ask your audience directly about what content they want to see. Polling is an easy way to get quick feedback and gauge interest in a particular topic.

- **Example Poll Question**: "Which video would you prefer to see next: 'How to Make Vegan Ice Cream' or '5 Quick Vegan Recipes for Busy People'?"
- **Monitor Engagement**: Track the number of responses and the level of engagement to understand what content your audience is most excited about.

Analyze Comments and Messages

Pay attention to the **comments** section of your existing videos. Often, viewers will leave suggestions or ask questions that can spark new content ideas. If people are repeatedly asking for a tutorial on a specific topic, that's a great indication that there's interest.

Look at Social Media

Check the conversations happening on social media platforms like Twitter, Facebook, and Reddit. Join relevant groups or forums in your niche and observe what questions or challenges people are discussing. This can help you uncover pain points or areas where your content can provide value.

Check Analytics

YouTube's **Analytics** is a goldmine for understanding what's working and what isn't. Look at which videos have the highest **watch time**, **engagement**, and **click-through rates**. If certain types of videos are performing better, this can guide your content strategy moving forward.

- **Audience Retention**: If viewers are watching your videos for longer, it means they're interested in the topic.
- **Traffic Sources**: See where your views are coming from. If you're getting lots of traffic from **search** or **suggested videos**, it's an indication that your content aligns well with what people are looking for.

Outlining Your First Video Series

Creating a video series on YouTube can be a game-changer for your channel's growth and engagement. While standalone videos have their place, a well-thought-out series can offer a deeper connection with your audience, encourage repeat views, and help build anticipation for your content. In this chapter, we'll explore the benefits of creating a series versus standalone videos, how to plan 3-5 video topics for consistency, and how to storyboard your ideas to ensure clarity and a cohesive narrative throughout your series.

1. Benefits of Creating a Series vs. Standalone Videos

Creating a video series instead of a collection of standalone videos can have several advantages that can help you grow your channel, boost engagement, and retain viewers for longer periods.

Increased Viewer Retention

One of the primary benefits of a video series is that it encourages **viewers to return** for subsequent episodes. When you create a series, each video becomes part of a larger narrative or theme, and viewers who enjoyed the first video are more likely to watch the next one to continue the journey. This leads to **higher watch time** and better **viewer retention rates**, which are important factors for YouTube's algorithm.

Example: If you create a cooking channel, a series like "Beginner's Guide to Vegan Cooking" can entice viewers to come back each week for new tips, recipes, and advice.

Building Anticipation

By establishing a series, you give your audience something to look forward to. Unlike standalone videos, where viewers may watch once and then move on, a series can create **anticipation** and **excitement** for upcoming episodes. When viewers are invested in the story or theme you're sharing, they're more likely to engage with the content over time.

Example: A tech reviewer might create a series like "Building My Dream PC," where each episode is about a different stage of the build, from selecting parts to assembly, which keeps viewers excited for the next step.

Strengthening Your Niche

A series allows you to go deeper into a specific subject, providing **value** and **expertise** to your audience. By focusing on a specific topic over multiple videos, you can establish yourself as an authority in your niche. This approach not only enhances your credibility but also helps attract a more targeted audience.

Example: A fitness channel might create a series like "10 Days to Better Flexibility," where each day's video builds on the last, creating an opportunity for you to address a specific goal, step by step.

Stronger Content Structure

A series provides you with a clear structure for your content, ensuring that your videos flow well together and that your channel has a more cohesive feel. This is in contrast to standalone videos, which may feel disconnected or random. The organized structure of a series can help make your content feel more polished and professional.

2. Planning 3-5 Video Topics for Consistency

When you start brainstorming for your video series, consistency is key. A successful series is one that feels like it's progressing or building upon itself, keeping viewers engaged from episode to episode. Here's how to plan 3-5 video topics to ensure consistency:

Choose a Central Theme or Topic

The first step in planning your series is to decide on a central theme or topic that will tie your videos together. This theme should be something that excites you and aligns with your niche, while also being broad enough to provide several subtopics for multiple episodes.
Examples:

- **Tech Channel**: "How to Build a Budget Gaming PC" (You can break this down into episodes like selecting components, assembly, software installation, and performance testing.)
- **Beauty Channel**: "Ultimate Skincare Routine" (Each video can focus on a different step in a comprehensive routine, such as cleansing, toning, moisturizing, etc.)
- **Travel Channel**: "Exploring Local Cuisine Around the World" (Each episode could highlight a different country's food culture and signature dishes.)

Outline Your Episodes

Once you have your central theme, start brainstorming 3-5 video topics that will make up your series. Think about the natural progression of your content—what topics make sense to cover next after one episode? Each video should be able to stand on its own but also flow into the next.

Example: For a "How to Start a YouTube Channel" series, the videos could be structured as:

1. Episode 1: *Choosing Your Niche and Setting Up Your Channel*
2. Episode 2: *Creating Your First Video: Filming and Editing Basics*
3. Episode 3: *Optimizing Your YouTube Channel for Success*
4. Episode 4: *Growing Your Audience: Marketing and Social Media Strategies*
5. Episode 5: *Monetizing Your Channel and Earning Revenue*

This approach ensures that each episode builds on the previous one, while still offering value to viewers who may join the series at any point.

Focus on Viewer Engagement

Think about how each video can engage viewers and make them excited for the next episode. You can incorporate **call-to-action statements,** like "Be sure to subscribe so you don't miss next week's video" or "Let me know in the comments if you'd like me to cover a specific topic in the next episode." This interaction not only boosts engagement but also gives you insight into what your viewers are interested in.

3. Storyboarding Your Ideas for Clarity

Once you've planned out the structure and topics of your series, it's time to refine your ideas through **storyboarding**. Storyboarding is a great way to visualize the flow of your videos, ensuring that your content is clear, organized, and engaging.

What Is a Storyboard?

A storyboard is a **visual representation** of each video in your series. It outlines the key scenes, shots, and transitions that will take place, ensuring that you have a clear plan for how to convey your message. You don't need to be an artist to create a storyboard—simple sketches or written descriptions can help you map out the content of your videos.

Steps to Create a Storyboard:

1. **Break Down the Video**: Start by breaking down each episode into its main components. What are the key segments of the video? (e.g., Introduction, Main Content, Call to Action, Outro).
2. **Outline Shots and Transitions**: Next, think about the types of shots you'll need for each segment—close-ups, wide shots, cutaways, etc. This will help you organize your filming process and ensure you don't miss any important moments.
3. **Add Visual and Audio Notes**: For each scene, note any important visual or audio elements. This could

include things like background music, on-screen text, or animations.
4. **Plan for B-Roll**: If your video will include B-roll (supplemental footage), plan where it will be inserted in the storyboard. B-roll is essential for keeping the video visually interesting and enhancing your message.

Storyboard Example:

- **Episode 1**: "Choosing Your Niche and Setting Up Your Channel"
- **Intro (Scene 1)**: On-camera introduction, explaining the importance of choosing the right niche. Show a quick B-roll of someone brainstorming ideas.
- **Main Content (Scene 2)**: Discuss different niche options, with on-screen text listing them. Include B-roll of different YouTube channels in those niches.
- **Outro (Scene 3)**: Recap, call to action to subscribe, and teaser for Episode 2. B-roll of a YouTube homepage, showing the "Subscribe" button.

Why Storyboarding Helps

Storyboarding helps you visualize the entire video before you start filming, making the editing process smoother and more efficient. It also ensures that each video in the series follows a cohesive structure and maintains clarity throughout.

Setting Up a Content Calendar

Creating and following a content calendar is one of the most powerful strategies for running a successful YouTube channel. Consistency is key to growing your audience, maintaining engagement, and keeping your creative energy flowing. A well-organized content calendar helps you stay on track, plan ahead, and avoid the stress that can come from scrambling to create content last minute. In this chapter, we'll explore the importance of consistent uploads, the best tools for scheduling and planning your content, and how to manage burnout by setting realistic timelines.

1. The Importance of Consistent Uploads

Consistency is one of the most important factors for success on YouTube. While the platform offers a wide range of opportunities, it is the creators who show up consistently who see the most significant growth in terms of both audience size and engagement.

Why Consistency Matters

- **Building Trust**: When viewers know that they can expect content from you regularly, they are more likely to subscribe and return. This builds a sense of trust and reliability, encouraging your audience to check in frequently.
- **YouTube's Algorithm**: Consistent uploads signal to YouTube's algorithm that you are an active creator. The algorithm favors channels that upload regularly because it shows that the creator is committed to providing valuable content. This results in higher visibility and more recommended content in search results and on viewers'

homepages.
- **Audience Engagement**: Regular uploads allow you to foster a deeper connection with your audience. The more often they see your content, the more familiar they become with your brand and style. This leads to **higher retention rates** and a stronger sense of community.

Examples of Consistent Uploading

- **Weekly Uploads**: A consistent weekly schedule works well for most creators. For example, a beauty channel might upload makeup tutorials every Tuesday at 5 PM, which helps the audience know when to expect the next video.
- **Bi-Weekly Uploads**: Some channels thrive on a bi-weekly schedule, especially if the content is more detailed or requires more time for editing. A tech channel might opt to release in-depth product reviews every two weeks instead of weekly.

How Consistency Impacts Growth

Consistency in uploading isn't just about quantity; it's about creating a rhythm that both you and your audience can depend on. For instance, posting once a week consistently is more beneficial than posting sporadically, even if the quality is high. A predictable content schedule gives viewers something to look forward to, and the repetition helps with brand recognition.

2. Tools for Scheduling and Planning

When it comes to planning and scheduling your content, there are several powerful tools that can help keep your content calendar organized, streamline your workflow, and ensure you stay on track with your publishing goals.

Google Calendar

Google Calendar is a simple yet effective tool for scheduling content. You can set reminders for when each video needs to be filmed, edited, and uploaded. This helps keep you organized and allows you to visualize your content plan for the month or quarter.

- **How to Use Google Calendar**: Create separate calendars for different stages of your video production (e.g., Scripting, Filming, Editing, Uploading). Color-code each stage to make it easy to identify at a glance. Set reminders for each step to ensure that you stay ahead of your deadlines.

Trello

Trello is a fantastic tool for organizing and tracking content ideas. With Trello, you can create different boards for each content topic and track the status of each video from concept to publication.

- **How to Use Trello**: Create lists for each stage of video production (e.g., "Ideas," "Scripting," "Filming," "Editing," and "Uploaded"). Within each list, create cards for individual video topics. You can add due dates, checklists, and collaborate with team members if needed. Trello also integrates with tools like Google Drive and Dropbox, which makes file management easier.

Notion

Notion is a versatile app that allows you to create customized content calendars, task lists, and wikis for your channel. It's an all-in-one tool that can be used to organize video ideas, deadlines, scripts, and even content performance tracking.

- **How to Use Notion**: Set up a content calendar with databases to track your upcoming videos, including titles, deadlines, and a status column to track progress. Notion also allows you to store research, ideas, and reference material for each video in one place.

Social Media Scheduling Tools

For channels that heavily rely on social media promotion, tools like **Buffer** or **Hootsuite** can help you schedule posts in advance. This ensures that you're actively promoting your content without having to worry about it every day.

- **How to Use Buffer/Hootsuite**: Schedule posts for Instagram, Twitter, Facebook, and more. You can plan your content around your video releases, ensuring your audience is consistently engaged on multiple platforms, driving traffic to your YouTube channel.

3. Managing Burnout with Realistic Timelines

While consistency is important, it's equally important to avoid **burnout**. Overloading yourself with an unrealistic posting schedule or trying to produce too much content at once can quickly lead to exhaustion and a decline in the quality of your videos. The key is to **find a sustainable pace** that balances your creative energy with your overall life responsibilities.

Setting Realistic Timelines

Before committing to a posting schedule, assess how much time you realistically have to dedicate to creating content each week. Consider your other commitments, like work, school, or personal life. Setting achievable goals will help you avoid the pressure that often leads to burnout.

- **Example**: If you can realistically dedicate 10 hours per week to creating content, try to aim for one video every two weeks rather than attempting to upload weekly. Gradually, you can increase your output as your workflow becomes more efficient.

Batch Filming and Editing

Batch filming is a great way to stay ahead of your content creation. Instead of filming one video at a time, try to shoot multiple videos in one sitting. This helps maximize your time and ensures you have videos ready to go when you need them. Similarly, you can batch edit your videos in advance, ensuring you always have content in the pipeline.

- **How to Use Batch Filming**: Choose a day to film 2-4 videos in one sitting. This way, you're not scrambling to film every week, and you can focus your editing time on multiple projects at once.

Setting Boundaries

It's important to recognize when you need a break. Create **buffer zones** between your content creation days to recharge your energy and avoid creative fatigue. Having breaks between video production allows you to return with fresh ideas and enthusiasm.

- **Example**: If you release a video every week, consider taking a week off every 4-6 weeks to recharge, review analytics, or work on bigger projects that require more time.

Flexible Timelines

Life happens, and sometimes you might fall behind on your content plan. It's crucial to allow for flexibility within your content calendar. Having some breathing room in your schedule gives you the freedom to adjust when things don't go as planned without feeling pressured.

- **Example**: If you plan to upload on Fridays, but you realize that you need more time for editing or life events come up, you can adjust your upload day to the following week, without it being detrimental to your overall strategy.

Section 3: Preparing Your Equipment and Tools

In this section, we'll help you choose the right gear and software to start making professional-quality videos without a huge upfront investment.

Choosing Basic Equipment

When starting a YouTube channel, one of the most important considerations is the equipment you'll use to create your videos. You might think you need a large budget to create professional-quality content, but that's not the case. In this chapter, we'll explore **basic equipment** options that will help you get started without breaking the bank. We'll cover camera options, audio considerations, and lighting setups, all of which are key to producing high-quality content that resonates with your audience.

1. Camera Options for Beginners

The camera is the centerpiece of your video production setup, and it's important to choose one that suits your budget and content style. Fortunately, there are several options available for beginners that can deliver excellent results.

Smartphones: The All-in-One Solution

For many beginners, the **smartphone** is the perfect starting point. Modern smartphones come with impressive cameras that can record in high-definition (HD) or even 4K, making them a convenient and affordable choice for new YouTubers.

- **Advantages of Smartphones**:
- **Portability**: Easy to carry around and use in various environments.
- **Good Quality**: Many smartphones have excellent cameras, even on lower-end models. Most offer HD video recording at 1080p or 4K quality.
- **User-Friendly**: With minimal setup, you can start recording right away. Plus, smartphones typically come with built-in stabilization and autofocus, which helps ensure smooth footage.
- **What You Need**:
- **Tripod**: A sturdy tripod designed for smartphones will help stabilize your shots. Look for one with adjustable heights and angles.
- **External Lenses**: If you want to expand your smartphone's capabilities, you can use external lenses to improve the camera's focus, zoom, and wide-angle capabilities.
- **Smartphone Camera Apps**: There are also camera apps available that allow you to manually control settings like focus, exposure, and ISO for a more professional look.

Webcams: Simple and Effective for Talk-Style Videos

If your content revolves around talking to the camera (e.g., vlogs, tutorials, reviews), a **webcam** could be a good option. Webcams are great for indoor setups and offer a consistent, plug-and-play solution.

- **Advantages of Webcams**:

- **Affordable**: Webcams are typically budget-friendly and offer good video quality at 720p or 1080p resolution.
- **Ease of Use**: Plug the webcam into your computer, and you're good to go. No need for additional equipment or setup.
- **Built-in Features**: Many webcams offer features like auto-focus, auto-light correction, and even noise reduction.
- **What You Need**:
- **Tripod or Mount**: Ensure your webcam is set up at the right angle for your videos, and consider getting a tripod or a mounting arm for added flexibility.

DSLR or Mirrorless Cameras: Professional-Quality Footage

If you're looking for a more professional look and feel, a **DSLR** or **mirrorless camera** is a great investment. These cameras deliver exceptional video quality, depth of field (blurry backgrounds), and greater control over settings like exposure, focus, and ISO.

- **Advantages of DSLRs/Mirrorless Cameras**:
- **Superior Image Quality**: These cameras offer high-definition video and allow you to shoot in 4K. You'll also get beautiful depth of field effects (blurry background) that make your videos look more cinematic.
- **Interchangeable Lenses**: You can switch lenses to achieve different looks. For example, a wide-angle lens can capture more of the background, while a prime lens can help with sharp focus.
- **Manual Controls**: DSLRs and mirrorless cameras give you full control over settings like white balance, ISO,

shutter speed, and aperture, helping you fine-tune the look of your videos.
- **What You Need**:
- **Lens**: Beginners should look for lenses with wide apertures (like f/1.8 or f/2.8) for good low-light performance and a blurred background effect.
- **Tripod**: A sturdy tripod is a must for keeping the camera steady during filming.
- **SD Card**: A large-capacity SD card is necessary to store your video files.

Choosing the Right Camera for You

Ultimately, the camera you choose depends on your content type and budget. If you're just starting, **smartphones** and **webcams** are fantastic options that can get you started with minimal investment. If you're more committed to long-term growth and higher production value, **DSLRs** or **mirrorless cameras** might be worth considering.

2. Audio Considerations

Audio is just as important as video quality. Poor audio can drive viewers away, even if the video itself is visually appealing. Clear, crisp sound is essential for keeping your audience engaged.

Built-in Camera Microphones

Most cameras come with **built-in microphones**, but they tend to pick up background noise, create echo, or sound muffled. These microphones are fine for casual videos, but if you want to take your audio quality to the next level, you'll want to invest in an **external microphone**.

External Microphones: A Game Changer

Investing in a good external microphone can drastically improve your audio quality. Here are a few popular types:

- **Lavalier Microphones**: These clip-on microphones are a great choice if you're recording yourself while moving around. They're small, portable, and often come with a long cable. Many YouTubers use them for talking-head videos or when they're filming outdoors.
- **Shotgun Microphones**: These are directional microphones that pick up sound from a specific area in front of you. Shotgun mics are ideal for recording high-quality audio without capturing too much background noise. They are great for both indoor and outdoor recording.
- **USB Microphones**: These are plug-and-play microphones that connect directly to your computer. Popular models like the **Blue Yeti** or **Audio-Technica AT2020** offer excellent sound quality and are easy to set up.

Soundproofing Your Recording Space

To improve audio quality even further, you may want to consider soundproofing your recording environment. Background noise can be distracting and lower the overall production value of your videos.

- **Soundproofing Tips**:
- **Soft Materials**: Use carpets, rugs, or curtains to absorb sound. You can also add foam panels or acoustic tiles to reduce echo and noise reflections.
- **Quiet Environment**: Record in a quiet space, away from busy streets or noisy appliances. Close windows and doors to minimize sound interference.

3. Lighting Setups for Better Video Quality

Good lighting is one of the easiest ways to make your videos look more professional. Proper lighting can enhance your appearance, eliminate shadows, and ensure that your videos are bright and clear.

Natural Light: The Budget-Friendly Option

If you're filming at home and on a budget, **natural light** is your best friend. Set up near a large window with plenty of sunlight, and position yourself facing the light source. This will help create a soft, flattering look that is great for beginners.

- **What to Keep in Mind**:
- Try to shoot when the light is soft, such as during the early

morning or late afternoon, to avoid harsh shadows.
- Be mindful of the weather, as it can drastically change the quality of natural light. On cloudy days, the light will be softer and more diffused, while bright sunlight may create strong shadows.

Ring Lights: A Popular Solution

If you need more control over your lighting, a **ring light** is an excellent option. Ring lights are widely used by YouTubers and influencers because they provide soft, even lighting that reduces shadows on your face.

- **Why Ring Lights are Great**:
- **Even Light**: The circular design ensures that the light is evenly distributed, giving you a well-lit and flattering look.
- **Adjustable**: Many ring lights come with adjustable brightness settings and color temperature controls, allowing you to tailor the lighting to suit your needs.
- **How to Use**: Position the ring light directly in front of you, with the camera in the center of the ring. This setup minimizes harsh shadows and creates a bright, professional look.

Softbox Lighting: For Professional Quality

For a more sophisticated setup, you can use **softbox lights**. These provide diffused light, which eliminates harsh shadows and creates a professional look, particularly for videos where you need bright, clear lighting for your face.

- **Advantages of Softboxes**:
- They are ideal for creating even, diffused lighting that makes you look polished on camera.
- Softboxes often come with adjustable stands and can be placed on either side of you to create a balanced, flattering effect.
- **How to Use**: Position one softbox on either side of you, angled towards your face to create a balanced, well-lit look. If you want a more dramatic effect, you can adjust the intensity and placement of the lights.

Essential Software for YouTube Success

Once you've set up your YouTube channel and started recording your videos, the next step is editing, designing, and tracking your progress. While the right **hardware** is crucial, **software** plays an equally important role in refining your content and ensuring your channel's growth. In this chapter, we will explore the essential software tools you'll need for video editing, creating eye-catching thumbnails, and tracking your channel's performance. Let's dive into the world of editing, design, and analytics software.

1. Video Editing Tools for Beginners

Video editing is where your raw footage transforms into polished, engaging content. While there are many complex video editing programs available, beginners don't need to be overwhelmed. There are several **user-friendly tools** that make editing intuitive and fun without requiring extensive technical expertise.

iMovie (Mac)

For beginners using Apple devices, **iMovie** is an excellent starting point. It's intuitive and comes pre-installed on most MacBooks, iPhones, and iPads. Despite being beginner-friendly, iMovie offers a variety of features that can help you create professional-looking videos.

- **Key Features**:
- **Easy Drag-and-Drop Interface**: You can quickly place clips, transitions, and music with simple drag-and-drop actions.
- **Pre-set Templates**: iMovie offers pre-built templates that make editing faster, such as cinematic trailers and themed intros.
- **Basic Effects**: You can add text, transitions, and simple color corrections, allowing you to enhance your video without much effort.
- **When to Use**: If you're just starting out and have a Mac device, iMovie is perfect for basic editing needs and simple projects. It's great for cutting, trimming, and adding music to your videos.

Shotcut (Windows, Mac, Linux)

If you're looking for a free, open-source video editor with more advanced features, **Shotcut** is a fantastic option. Available for Windows, Mac, and Linux, Shotcut supports a wide range of video formats and includes multiple video tracks, effects, and transitions.

- **Key Features**:
- **Cross-Platform**: Works on multiple operating systems without requiring an expensive software license.
- **Advanced Features for Beginners**: It includes features like video filters, transitions, and color correction, but doesn't overwhelm you with too many options.
- **Customizable Interface**: You can adjust the layout and toolbars to suit your editing style.
- **When to Use**: If you're a beginner on a budget but want to access more professional tools, Shotcut is an excellent choice. It's perfect for creating YouTube content with an upgrade in production value.

Adobe Premiere Rush (Windows, Mac, iOS, Android)

For those who want the power of Adobe Premiere Pro without the complexity, **Adobe Premiere Rush** is a solid alternative. It's a mobile-friendly version of Premiere Pro designed for YouTube creators and beginners.

- **Key Features**:
- **User-Friendly**: The layout is simple, and it offers drag-and-drop functionality, making it easy for beginners to pick up.
- **Cross-Device Sync**: You can start editing on your phone and continue on your desktop without missing a beat.
- **Essential Editing Tools**: It offers color correction, audio editing, text overlays, and transitions, allowing you to produce polished videos with ease.

- **When to Use**: If you need something lightweight and mobile-friendly but still want access to a professional suite of tools, Premiere Rush is perfect for editing videos on-the-go.

DaVinci Resolve (Windows, Mac, Linux)

If you want a more advanced option, **DaVinci Resolve** is a free video editing software with powerful features used by professionals. While the learning curve is steeper compared to iMovie or Shotcut, DaVinci Resolve provides exceptional control over color grading, audio mixing, and video editing.

- **Key Features**:
- **Color Grading**: DaVinci Resolve is known for its high-quality color grading, giving your videos a cinematic look.
- **Multi-Track Editing**: You can layer audio and video tracks, which is useful for complex editing projects.
- **Free Version**: The free version offers a range of features without limitations, but there's also a paid version if you want more advanced tools.
- **When to Use**: If you're ready to dive into more advanced editing and need precise control over your video's look and feel, DaVinci Resolve is ideal.

2. Graphic Design Tools for Thumbnails

Thumbnails are one of the most important elements of your YouTube content. A good thumbnail can drastically increase your click-through rate (CTR), and with the right tools, you can create eye-catching designs without needing to be a graphic design expert.

Canva (Web, iOS, Android)

Canva is a popular, user-friendly tool for creating professional-looking thumbnails, even if you have no design experience. It offers templates specifically for YouTube thumbnails, making it easier than ever to create something eye-catching in minutes.

- **Key Features**:
- **Templates**: Canva offers a variety of pre-made YouTube thumbnail templates that you can customize with your images, text, and colors.
- **Drag-and-Drop Interface**: The simple interface makes it easy to add elements to your thumbnail like text, icons, and shapes.
- **Free and Paid Versions**: The free version offers plenty of features, but the Pro version gives you access to more advanced tools and a wider selection of assets.
- **When to Use**: If you're a beginner and want a quick, easy way to create thumbnails without spending a lot of time on design, Canva is perfect.

Adobe Spark (Web, iOS, Android)

Another great tool for creating YouTube thumbnails is **Adobe Spark**, which offers a wide range of templates and design elements. It's especially useful if you're already familiar with Adobe's ecosystem but need a more beginner-friendly option.

- **Key Features**:

- **Customizable Templates**: Choose from a variety of YouTube thumbnail templates and personalize them with your images and text.
- **Built-In Stock Photos**: Access thousands of free and premium stock photos to enhance your thumbnails.
- **Easy Integration**: If you're using other Adobe products, Adobe Spark integrates seamlessly into your workflow.
- **When to Use**: If you need more design flexibility and are comfortable using Adobe products, Adobe Spark is a great choice for designing thumbnails quickly and easily.

PicMonkey (Web, iOS, Android)

PicMonkey is another graphic design tool for beginners that's perfect for creating custom thumbnails. With a focus on simplicity and ease of use, PicMonkey offers drag-and-drop functionality and various templates.

- **Key Features**:
- **Photo Editing Tools**: You can enhance your thumbnails with effects, filters, and touch-up features.
- **Customizable Text and Graphics**: Add engaging text and elements that help your thumbnails stand out.
- **Easy Interface**: The interface is clean and easy to navigate, which helps beginners design high-quality thumbnails quickly.
- **When to Use**: If you want a straightforward tool for designing thumbnails with a bit more flexibility than Canva, PicMonkey is a solid choice.

3. Analytics Tools for Tracking Progress

As you grow your YouTube channel, understanding how your videos are performing is essential for continued success. Using **analytics tools** can help you track your growth, identify trends, and optimize your content for better results.

YouTube Studio

YouTube's built-in analytics tool, **YouTube Studio**, is an essential resource for tracking the performance of your videos and channel. It's completely free, and you can access detailed data right from your dashboard.

- **Key Features**:
- **Video Analytics**: Track key metrics such as watch time, views, likes, and comments on individual videos.
- **Audience Insights**: Understand who your audience is, including their age, gender, and location.
- **Revenue Reports**: If you're monetized, YouTube Studio provides insights into your earnings, including ad revenue, Super Chats, and memberships.
- **When to Use**: YouTube Studio should be your primary analytics tool. It's easy to use and gives you all the data you need to understand your channel's performance.

Google Analytics

Although primarily used for websites, **Google Analytics** can also be connected to your YouTube channel to track traffic sources, audience demographics, and user behavior outside of

YouTube.

- **Key Features**:
- **Traffic Source Tracking**: Understand where your traffic is coming from, whether it's from YouTube search, external websites, or social media.
- **Audience Behavior**: Get detailed insights into how users engage with your content, such as the average time spent on videos and bounce rates.
- **When to Use**: Use Google Analytics if you're managing multiple platforms and need a broader view of how people are interacting with your content across the web.

TubeBuddy

For YouTubers looking for in-depth insights and tools beyond what YouTube Studio provides, **TubeBuddy** is a powerful browser extension designed specifically for creators. TubeBuddy offers a wide range of features to help with optimization, keyword research, and tracking.

- **Key Features**:
- **Keyword Research**: TubeBuddy helps you find the best keywords for your videos, improving your SEO and increasing discoverability.
- **Tag Suggestions**: TubeBuddy provides tag suggestions for your videos, helping you rank higher in search results.
- **Video Analytics**: TubeBuddy gives you deeper insights into the performance of your videos and suggests ways to improve your content.
- **When to Use**: If you're serious about growing your

channel and want additional tools to help optimize your content and track performance, TubeBuddy is a fantastic resource.

Creating a Starter Studio on a Budget

When starting your YouTube journey, one of the most common concerns is **setting up your filming space** without breaking the bank. You don't need to spend thousands of dollars on equipment to create professional-looking videos. With a little creativity and strategic planning, you can build a functional and efficient **home studio** on a budget. This chapter will guide you through setting up your filming space, improving your audio and video quality with DIY hacks, and organizing your workspace for maximum efficiency.

1. Setting Up Your Filming Space at Home

Creating a filming space at home doesn't require a dedicated room or large budget. The key is **optimizing your existing space** to suit your needs, and there are many ways to do this without spending a fortune.

Choosing the Right Location

The first step is to identify where you'll be filming. While you might not have a professional studio, you can **make use of any available space** in your home. Here are some factors to consider:

- **Natural Lighting**: Choose a spot with **good natural lighting**, preferably near a window. Natural light is free and can make your videos look more vibrant and inviting. Position yourself facing the window or slightly to the side to avoid harsh shadows.
- **Background**: Keep your background clean and uncluttered. If you don't have a dedicated backdrop, consider using a plain wall or creating a simple setup with decorations, plants, or bookshelves. **DIY backdrops** (such as a plain curtain or fabric) can add a professional touch without the need for an expensive setup.
- **Quiet Space**: Find a space in your home that's free from background noise. A quiet room will help ensure that your audio quality remains clear, which is just as important as good video.

Space Optimization

If space is limited, look for ways to optimize your area without cluttering it. Use **foldable furniture** or **portable equipment** that can be easily set up and put away when you're done filming. A **small corner** can be transformed into a makeshift studio if you make good use of the space.

2. DIY Hacks for Improving Audio and Video Quality

You don't need expensive equipment to improve the quality of your videos. There are plenty of **affordable DIY solutions** that can significantly enhance your production value, especially when it comes to **audio** and **video**.

DIY Audio Hacks

Clear, crisp audio is crucial for YouTube videos, and luckily, you don't have to break the bank to get good sound. Here are a few budget-friendly tips to improve your audio:

- **Use a Lapel Mic or Smartphone Microphone**: If you don't have a professional microphone, **lapel microphones** (also called lap mics) are a budget-friendly option that offers great audio quality for talking-head videos. You can also use your **smartphone's headphone mic** as an affordable alternative to high-end microphones.
- **Reduce Background Noise**: To improve audio quality, minimize any potential noise in your filming space. Use **soft materials** like pillows, blankets, or curtains to absorb sound and reduce echo. You can even **hang a blanket** on the wall behind you to create a more soundproof environment.
- **DIY Pop Filter**: If you're using a regular microphone and notice **popping sounds** when speaking (like harsh "P" sounds), you can create a simple **pop filter**. Stretch a piece of **pantyhose** over a coat hanger or a plastic circle and attach it in front of your microphone. This will help soften the sounds and improve overall audio quality.

DIY Video Hacks

Your video quality can make a big difference in how professional your content looks. You don't need a high-end camera to get great footage, but with some **simple hacks**, you can improve the video quality.

- **Lighting on a Budget**: Good lighting is essential for clear, well-lit videos. If you're not ready to invest in professional lights, here are a few affordable solutions:
- Use a **softbox DIY light** made with a white sheet or tissue paper to diffuse light from a lamp, creating a soft glow.
- **Ring lights** are an affordable way to provide even lighting. You can even use **LED desk lamps** with adjustable brightness to set up your lighting.
- Place **reflective surfaces** (such as white foam boards or whiteboards) to bounce light and reduce shadows.
- **Smartphone for Filming**: You don't need an expensive DSLR camera to create high-quality content. Many modern smartphones have great cameras that can shoot in 1080p or even 4K. Use your phone with a **tripod** or **phone mount** to keep your shots steady and professional.
- **Stabilize Your Shots**: If you're filming without a tripod, you can stabilize your camera by using household items like **books or boxes** to rest your phone or camera on. Alternatively, consider using a **gimbal stabilizer** (an affordable option is available for smartphones) to achieve smooth, cinematic footage.
- **DIY Diffusers and Reflectors**: Instead of buying expensive diffusers or reflectors, use materials like **white bedsheets**, **shower curtains**, or **poster boards** to diffuse light or reflect it back onto your face, softening shadows and ensuring you look great on camera.

3. Organizing Your Workspace for Efficiency

Now that you have your filming space set up and your DIY hacks in place, it's time to think about **organizing your workspace**. A clean, well-organized studio can make a huge difference in how efficiently you work, which is crucial when you're managing a YouTube channel.

Create a Dedicated Filming Area

Try to set up a dedicated area in your home for filming and storing your equipment. This doesn't have to be a huge space, but **designating a specific corner** or area for your YouTube work will help you stay focused and efficient.

- **Storage Solutions**: Use **storage bins**, **shelves**, or **drawers** to keep your equipment organized and easily accessible. If you have multiple pieces of gear like lights, microphones, or tripods, create a storage system to avoid clutter and keep everything in one place.
- **Cable Management**: Keep cables organized by using **cable ties** or **Velcro strips** to bundle wires and prevent them from tangling. This will help you quickly set up your equipment without wasting time untangling cables every time you film.

Efficient Setup and Breakdown

If your filming space is small or multi-purpose, consider creating a **quick setup and breakdown system**. Use portable equipment that's easy to assemble and store away when not in use.

- **Mobile Filming Setup**: Consider investing in a **foldable tripod** and **light stands** that can be easily collapsed and stored. If you need to move your filming setup between spaces, ensure that your gear is lightweight and easy to transport.
- **Pre-Plan Your Shot**: Before you start filming, make sure everything is in its proper place. Take a few minutes to **arrange your background, check the lighting**, and ensure the audio equipment is ready. This will save you time during filming and editing.

4

Chapter 3: Creating and Editing Your First Video

Section 1: Writing and Planning Your First Script

The process of creating your first video begins before you even hit record. A well-thought-out script can make all the difference in how engaging and clear your video will be. This section will guide you through writing an effective script that connects with your audience.

Structuring Your Video

The structure of your YouTube video plays a crucial role in capturing and retaining your audience's attention. Whether you're creating a tutorial, a vlog, or an educational piece, how you organize your video can make a significant difference in how well it resonates with viewers and how likely they are to take the desired actions afterward. This chapter will break down the essential components of a well-structured video: starting with a captivating **hook**, delivering valuable content in the middle, and wrapping up with a **strong call to action**.

1. The Importance of a Hook in the Introduction

The introduction of your video sets the tone for the rest of the content. It's the first few moments that will either hook the viewer in or cause them to click away. A great hook draws your audience in, grabs their attention, and makes them want to stick around for more.

What is a Hook?

A hook is an attention-grabbing element you use at the beginning of your video to make viewers interested and curious about what's coming next. The purpose is to engage the audience immediately so that they don't scroll past your video or click away.

Types of Hooks

Here are several types of hooks you can use in the introduction to quickly capture your audience's attention:

- **Ask a Provocative Question**: Begin by asking a question that speaks directly to the viewer's needs, interests, or pain points. For example, "Are you tired of spending hours editing your YouTube videos?"
- **Tease the Value**: Give a sneak peek of what the viewer will learn or gain by watching the video. For instance, "In

this video, I'm going to show you a 5-minute trick that will instantly improve your editing skills."
- **Create Curiosity**: Use an intriguing statement that piques the viewer's interest and makes them want to know more. An example might be, "I almost quit YouTube because of this one mistake… but then I found a simple solution."
- **Start with a Bold Statement or Statistic**: Use an unexpected fact or statistic to surprise and engage your audience. "Did you know that 80% of YouTubers give up after their first year? I'm here to show you how to avoid that fate."

Why the Hook is Crucial

The hook serves as your **first impression**—it's the reason people will choose to watch your video instead of scrolling to the next one. Without a compelling hook, your audience may lose interest in the first few seconds. Your goal is to immediately demonstrate value, so viewers feel like they're in the right place.

2. Delivering Valuable Content in the Middle

Once you've got their attention, it's time to deliver the main content of your video. This is where you build on the promise you made in your introduction, providing information, entertainment, or education that is relevant and valuable to your audience. The middle section is where your viewers are deciding if they want to stick around until the end, so it's important to make every moment count.

Organizing the Middle Section

When structuring the middle of your video, it's important to **break it down into clear sections** to ensure your content flows smoothly and doesn't overwhelm the viewer. Consider the following approach:

- **Divide Content into Digestible Segments**: If your video covers multiple points, break them up into smaller sections. This makes the content easier to follow and prevents information overload. For example, if you're sharing 5 tips, introduce each tip clearly and give examples.
- **Stay Focused on the Topic**: Stick to the topic you promised in your hook and introduction. Providing **focused, actionable content** is key to keeping your audience engaged. Avoid going off on tangents, as this can lead to viewer drop-off.
- **Use Visuals to Enhance Understanding**: Support your content with **visual aids**, such as slides, on-screen text, graphs, or demonstrations. Visuals help reinforce your message and keep viewers engaged.
- **Keep the Pace Moving**: Maintain a consistent pace throughout the middle section of the video. Don't dwell too long on any single point, but don't rush through the content either. Find the balance between explaining your ideas clearly and keeping the video moving forward.

Engagement Tactics for the Middle Section

In the middle of your video, you can also incorporate strategies to **boost engagement**:

- **Ask Viewers for Feedback**: Encourage comments by asking questions related to the topic. For example, "What do you think about this tip? Let me know in the comments below."
- **Incorporate Viewer Questions**: If you have an active community, you can incorporate viewer questions from previous videos or social media, making the content more interactive and personal.
- **Storytelling**: Incorporating anecdotes or personal experiences related to the topic can make the content more relatable and engaging. For example, "When I first started, I struggled with this exact issue, and here's how I fixed it…"

3. Ending with a Strong Call to Action

Now that you've provided valuable content, it's time to wrap up your video with a **call to action (CTA)**. This is where you encourage your audience to take the next step—whether that's subscribing to your channel, liking the video, following you on social media, or checking out other content.

Why a CTA is Important

A call to action is essential because it directs the audience on what to do next. Without it, viewers may enjoy your content but might not take any action afterward, making it harder for you to grow your channel or build an engaged community.

Types of Calls to Action

Here are several effective calls to action you can use at the end of your video:

- **Subscribe to Your Channel**: Encourage viewers to subscribe for more content. For example, "If you found this video helpful, don't forget to hit that subscribe button for more tips!"
- **Engage in the Comments**: Ask viewers to comment with their thoughts, opinions, or questions. "I'd love to hear your thoughts on this tip! Drop a comment below and let me know what works best for you."
- **Watch Another Video**: Encourage viewers to continue watching by directing them to related content. "If you enjoyed this video, you'll love my next one on how to edit like a pro—click here to watch it now!"
- **Follow on Social Media**: Direct viewers to connect with you on other platforms. "For behind-the-scenes content and updates, be sure to follow me on Instagram @YourName."
- **Download or Sign Up**: If you're promoting a product or service, provide a clear CTA. "Click the link in the description to download my free guide on how to grow

your YouTube channel!"

Effective CTA Tips

- **Be Clear and Direct**: A good CTA is specific and easy to follow. Instead of just saying "subscribe," give them a reason why they should. "Subscribe so you never miss an upload on how to improve your YouTube game."
- **Create Urgency**: Encourage viewers to act now by adding urgency. "Subscribe today and get access to exclusive content!"
- **Show Appreciation**: Always thank your viewers for their time. A simple "Thanks for watching" goes a long way in building rapport with your audience.

Scripting Tips for Beginners

Creating a YouTube video requires more than just hitting the record button. One of the most important aspects of video creation is crafting a **script** that guides your content in a way that feels natural, engaging, and authentic. As a beginner, you may feel unsure about how to create a script that resonates with your audience. Don't worry—scripting can be a fun and rewarding process, especially when you focus on a few key strategies.

In this chapter, we'll dive into some essential **scripting tips for beginners**, covering how to write conversationally and authentically, how to incorporate storytelling into your videos, and how to balance preparation with flexibility.

1. Writing Conversationally and Authentically

When you're scripting your videos, it's crucial to remember that YouTube is a personal platform. Viewers are more likely to engage with content that feels **genuine** and **relatable**. Writing in a **conversational tone** is one of the best ways to make your content feel approachable and authentic.

Why Conversational Writing Works

A conversational style feels more natural to your audience, as though you're speaking directly to them. It helps to build a **connection** and makes your content more **engaging**. You don't want your audience to feel like they're listening to a script being read word-for-word; instead, they should feel like they're having a friendly chat with you.

How to Write Conversationally

- **Use Simple, Everyday Language**: Avoid jargon or overly complicated phrases. Speak the way you would in a casual conversation with a friend. For example, instead of saying, "Let's examine the ramifications of this decision," say "Let's talk about what this means for you."
- **Write as You Speak**: Read your script aloud as you write it. If it sounds stiff or unnatural when spoken, rewrite it. You want the flow of your words to sound as though you're having an organic conversation, not reading off a page.
- **Use Personal Pronouns**: Using words like "you" and "we" creates a direct connection with your audience. Instead of

saying, "Viewers will find this tip helpful," say, "You'll find this tip helpful."
- **Add Informal Phrasing**: Phrases like "I want to show you," "Let me explain," or "Here's the thing" give a sense of **invitation** and **warmth**, which can make your video feel more friendly and engaging.

Example of Conversational Writing

Here's a before-and-after example to demonstrate the difference between formal and conversational writing:

- **Formal**: "In this video, we will be discussing the importance of consistency in building your YouTube channel."
- **Conversational**: "Today, I'm going to talk to you about why consistency is key to growing your YouTube channel."

2. Incorporating Storytelling into Your Videos

People love stories—they're engaging, memorable, and relatable. Storytelling can be a powerful tool to make your content more compelling and emotional, helping your audience connect with you on a deeper level. Including personal anecdotes or storytelling elements in your videos can enhance your message and make it more impactful.

Why Storytelling is Essential

Storytelling isn't just for movie directors or novelists. It's a strategy that can make any content more engaging. When you tell a story, you can **empathize with your viewers**, evoke emotions, and drive home important lessons or points. It's also an excellent way to make abstract concepts more **concrete** and **relatable**.

How to Incorporate Storytelling

- **Start with a Personal Story**: Relate to your audience by sharing a personal experience or anecdote that's relevant to your topic. This could be a moment when you struggled and overcame an obstacle or a breakthrough in your journey. Personal stories build **trust** and make your content more authentic.
- **Use the Classic Story Arc**: Structure your story with a clear beginning, middle, and end. Start by setting the scene, describe the challenge you faced or the lesson you learned, and then wrap it up by sharing the resolution or takeaway. This structure makes your content more engaging and easier to follow.
- **Show, Don't Just Tell**: Rather than just telling your audience something is important, show them why it matters. For example, instead of saying, "Building a community is important," tell a story about how building a community helped you solve a problem or achieve a goal.
- **Relate the Story to Your Audience**: Make sure the story is relevant to your target audience. If you're talking to beginner YouTubers, for example, share stories about your own early struggles or victories. This makes the content more relatable and less about you, and more about what the audience can learn from your experience.

Example of Storytelling in Action

- **Without Storytelling**: "You need to be consistent with your uploads to grow on YouTube."
- **With Storytelling**: "When I first started my channel, I uploaded videos sporadically—sometimes every week, sometimes every month. It wasn't until I committed to a consistent upload schedule that I saw any real growth. The difference it made was incredible, and here's why…"

3. Balancing Preparation with Flexibility

As a beginner, it's easy to think that your script has to be perfect or completely detailed. However, it's important to strike a balance between preparing your content and staying flexible. Over-preparing can make your delivery feel stiff, while under-preparing can lead to rambling or forgetting key points.

Why Balance is Important

A script provides a helpful roadmap for your video, but leaving room for flexibility will help you sound more natural and spontaneous. Flexibility allows you to adapt to the flow of the video and respond to the energy of your delivery or even comments from your audience.

How to Balance Preparation and Flexibility

- **Outline, Don't Overwrite**: Instead of writing every word, create an outline with bullet points that guide you through the key topics. This gives you structure while

leaving room for you to speak freely and adjust as needed.
- **Leave Space for Improvisation**: If you're discussing a topic you're passionate about or have a lot of experience in, feel free to improvise a bit. Add personal touches or expand on ideas that come to mind in the moment. This helps you stay **engaged** and makes your content feel **authentic**.
- **Practice and Refine**: If you're nervous about being too flexible, rehearse your script a few times. You can also use a teleprompter app for a smoother delivery, but always try to avoid reading word-for-word. Practicing will help you become more comfortable with the content, allowing you to flow more naturally on camera.
- **Adjust Based on Feedback**: Be open to making changes in future videos based on audience feedback. If viewers comment that they love when you go off-script or share more personal stories, you can incorporate those elements more frequently.

Example of Flexibility in Action

- **Over-prepared**: "In this video, I'll be discussing the top 5 strategies to grow your channel. First, I'll talk about SEO. Second, we'll cover thumbnails. After that, let's go into engagement, followed by consistency, and lastly, content ideas."
- **Balanced Preparation**: "Today, I'm going to share 5 strategies to help you grow your YouTube channel. The first one is SEO—let me tell you how I learned it the hard way...

Practicing and Rehearsing

When it comes to delivering a great YouTube video, practicing and rehearsing are just as crucial as writing the script itself. While your script might sound perfect on paper, the real magic happens when you bring it to life on camera. The best way to ensure you deliver your content with confidence, clarity, and energy is through consistent **practice and rehearsal**.

In this chapter, we will explore how to effectively **read your script aloud for flow and clarity**, **practice in front of a mirror or camera**, and **get feedback from friends or family**. These techniques will help you fine-tune your delivery and make your presentation feel natural and engaging.

1. Reading Your Script Aloud for Flow and Clarity

Reading your script aloud might seem simple, but it's one of the most effective ways to catch any awkward phrasing, unclear sentences, or lack of flow. When you read your script aloud, you're able to hear how your words sound in real-time, allowing you to identify areas that need improvement.

Why Reading Aloud is Important

- **Catch awkward phrasing**: What sounds good in writing may not always translate well when spoken. Reading aloud helps you identify sentences that are hard to say or feel unnatural.
- **Test the flow**: You can hear if your script has a good rhythm. Are there parts that drag on? Are some sections too short or choppy? You'll notice these issues when you

speak the words out loud.
- **Identify clarity issues**: Sometimes, when we write, we may skip over certain details or explanations, assuming they are clear. Reading aloud can help you spot moments where more clarification is needed.

How to Read Your Script Aloud

- **Speak Slowly and Clearly**: It's important not to rush through your script. Speaking slowly allows you to focus on pronunciation, expression, and rhythm. This also helps you identify areas where you may stumble or trip over words.
- **Focus on Pacing**: As you read, pay attention to how fast or slow you're speaking. Are there sections that feel too fast? You may need to add a pause or change the sentence structure to make it easier to say.
- **Mark Areas to Improve**: While reading aloud, use a pen or highlighter to mark sentences that feel clunky or difficult to pronounce. These are areas you may need to rework or simplify.

Example

- **Before reading aloud**: "It is highly recommended that you carefully consider your target audience to ensure the success of your video content."
- **After reading aloud**: "Make sure to think about your audience carefully if you want your videos to succeed." Reading aloud reveals that the first version was overly formal and cumbersome. The second version flows much more

naturally.

2. Practicing in Front of a Mirror or Camera

Once you've refined your script through reading aloud, the next step is to practice in front of a **mirror** or **camera**. This is the stage where you start to get comfortable with your physical presence, body language, and delivery.

Why Practicing in Front of a Mirror or Camera Helps

- **Observe your body language**: You can see how you carry yourself on camera. Are you slouching? Are you fidgeting? Practicing in front of a mirror helps you become more aware of your posture and movements.
- **Improve your facial expressions**: You can watch how your facial expressions align with your words. Are you smiling when appropriate? Do you look engaged or bored? A mirror allows you to check these details.
- **Build comfort with the camera**: For many beginners, speaking directly to a camera can feel intimidating. Practicing in front of a mirror or recording yourself helps you become more comfortable in front of the lens.
- **Improve your delivery**: You'll start to see where you can add emotion, change your tone, or increase your energy. Practice in front of a mirror helps you gauge how enthusiastic or genuine you appear, which is key for maintaining viewer engagement.

How to Practice in Front of a Mirror or Camera

- **Start with the Mirror**: Stand in front of a mirror and practice delivering your script. Pay attention to how your hands move, whether your facial expressions match your tone, and whether you're speaking with confidence. If you notice any awkwardness, adjust your posture or gestures.
- **Record Yourself**: Set up your camera or phone to record while you rehearse. Watching a video of yourself will give you a better perspective on how you come across. You may notice things you didn't realize, like overuse of filler words or nervous habits, that you can work on.
- **Re-watch and Adjust**: After recording, watch the video critically. Take note of what works well and what doesn't. If you feel like you could be more engaging, practice adding more energy or changing your delivery.

Example

Let's say you're practicing an introduction to a video. When watching the recording, you may realize that you're speaking too quickly, or your body language is stiff. By adjusting your tone, slowing down, and using more hand gestures, you'll improve your delivery and make the video feel more natural.

3. Getting Feedback from Friends or Family

One of the best ways to improve your delivery is to get **feedback** from others. Friends and family can offer constructive criticism, point out things you might have missed, and provide insights into how engaging your content is.

Why Feedback from Others is Valuable

- **Fresh perspective**: It's easy to become too focused on yourself and miss the bigger picture. Getting feedback from someone else provides a fresh perspective and new ideas.
- **Spot weaknesses**: Sometimes, we don't notice nervous tics, distracting behaviors, or unclear parts of our script. Having someone else watch can highlight these areas and help you refine your presentation.
- **Boosts confidence**: Hearing positive feedback from those you trust can boost your confidence and help you feel more comfortable when it's time to film for real.

How to Get Feedback

- **Ask for Specific Feedback**: Rather than asking, "Did you like it?" try asking specific questions like, "Did I sound natural?" or "Were there any parts where I seemed unclear or confusing?" This invites more constructive and detailed feedback.
- **Take Notes on Criticism**: Listen to feedback with an open mind. Even if it feels uncomfortable, take notes on what your friends or family say. This will help you improve and become a better speaker over time.
- **Iterate Based on Feedback**: Use the feedback to refine your script and delivery. If they mention that you come across as too serious or not engaging enough, adjust your tone and try again.

Example

Suppose you asked a family member to watch your practice session, and they mention that you seemed too quiet in certain parts. You can adjust by projecting your voice more and emphasizing key points in your script.

Section 2: Shooting Your First Video

Now that your script is ready, it's time to bring it to life on camera. In this section, we'll cover everything you need to know to film your first video like a pro.

Setting Up Your Filming Environment

The environment where you film your YouTube videos plays a critical role in the quality of your content. A good filming space not only ensures that your visuals and audio are clear and professional but also enhances your overall production value. This chapter will guide you through the essentials of setting up a filming environment that works for you, focusing on **choosing a quiet, well-lit space**, **positioning your camera and tripod**, and **checking your background for distractions**.

1. Choosing a Quiet, Well-Lit Space

The first and most important consideration when setting up your filming environment is to choose a space that is both **quiet** and **well-lit**. These two elements are crucial for creating videos that look and sound professional. Here's why:

Why Lighting and Sound Matter

- **Lighting**: Proper lighting is essential for making your videos look clear and well-lit. Without adequate lighting, your video might appear dark, grainy, or unappealing, which can negatively affect the viewer's experience. Natural light is the best option, but affordable artificial lights work well too.
- **Sound**: Good audio is just as important as good video. Background noise or echo can distract viewers and detract from your content. Choose a location where external noise is minimal, and where the acoustics won't distort your voice.

How to Choose the Right Space

- **Quiet Location**: Look for a room or area with minimal background noise. Close windows to avoid traffic sounds, and turn off noisy appliances like fans, air conditioners, or fridges. You want your viewers to focus on you, not background disturbances.
- **Natural Lighting**: Ideally, choose a room with **natural light** (preferably from a window) that illuminates your face. Filming in the morning or late afternoon provides

soft, flattering light. If natural light isn't available or sufficient, use **softbox lights** or **ring lights** positioned in front of you to ensure even lighting. Avoid harsh, direct sunlight, as it can cause unwanted shadows or overexposure.
- **Controlling Artificial Light**: If you're relying on artificial lighting, make sure the light is diffused and doesn't create sharp shadows. Soft, diffused lighting creates a more flattering and professional look. You can use inexpensive softboxes or LED panels to create this effect.

2. Positioning Your Camera and Tripod

Once you've found a suitable space, the next step is to properly position your **camera and tripod**. Proper placement of your camera ensures that your video is framed correctly, while the tripod provides stability to prevent shaky footage.

Why Camera Position Matters

- **Framing and Composition**: The way you position your camera directly affects how you are framed in the shot. A bad angle can make you look awkward or unprofessional, while a good angle will highlight your best features and keep the viewer's attention on you.
- **Stability**: Shaky footage can be distracting and make your video feel unpolished. Using a tripod ensures your camera remains steady and stable, even during longer recording sessions.

How to Position Your Camera and Tripod

- **Eye-Level Shot**: Your camera should be positioned at **eye level** to ensure the shot is natural. Position the camera so that it is directly facing you, at about the height of your eyes. This creates a more engaging and personable connection with the viewer.
- **Distance**: Make sure the camera is positioned at an appropriate distance to capture your upper body and face. Avoid standing too close to the camera, as this can create an unflattering effect, or too far away, which can make you appear distant or disconnected. Aim for a shot that frames your upper torso and head, with a little space above your head to give room for your expression.
- **Tripod Positioning**: Use a **tripod** to ensure the camera is stable. Position the tripod on a flat surface to avoid accidental tilts or movements. If you're filming in a tight space, a smaller, adjustable tripod may be a better option for flexibility.
- **Avoiding Camera Movement**: Once your camera is set up, refrain from touching it during filming to prevent any shakes. If you need to adjust the angle or zoom in, do so before you begin recording.

3. Checking Your Background for Distractions

Your **background** is often overlooked, but it can make a big difference in how professional your video looks. A cluttered or distracting background can pull attention away from you, the main subject. A clean, tidy background ensures that your audience stays focused on your content and message.

Why the Background is Important

- **Focus on You**: Your background should support your video's content, not compete with it. A clean, simple background ensures that viewers focus on what you're saying and not what's happening behind you.
- **Visual Appeal**: A well-thought-out background can enhance the aesthetic of your video. It can be a reflection of your personality or brand, helping create a more engaging atmosphere.

How to Check and Optimize Your Background

- **Clear and Tidy**: Ensure that there's no clutter or unnecessary items in the frame. If you're filming in a room with bookshelves, make sure they're neat, or even consider removing items that don't add to the video's theme.
- **Avoid Distracting Elements**: Look for anything in the background that might distract viewers. Items like bright lights, random objects, or moving backgrounds can steal attention. Even personal items like family photos, while meaningful, can be distracting unless they fit the vibe of your content.
- **Backdrop Options**: If you want to add some personality to your background, consider using a **backdrop**. This could be a simple fabric backdrop, a branded poster, or even an aesthetic bookshelf. Keep it simple but relevant to your content. Avoid overly busy or bold patterns that could draw too much attention.
- **Using Virtual Backgrounds**: If you're filming in a space that has unavoidable distractions, consider using a **virtual**

background (if you're using a webcam or a tool like Zoom). These can give your videos a clean, professional look without the need for a physical background change.

Example

Imagine filming a cooking video. A cluttered kitchen counter with piles of dishes in the background could distract your viewers from the recipe you're demonstrating. By clearing the counter, keeping it simple, and maybe adding a small plant or a bowl of ingredients, you create a more inviting, focused atmosphere for your content.

Filming Techniques for Beginners

As you step into the world of YouTube content creation, understanding the basic filming techniques is crucial for creating engaging and professional-looking videos. Whether you're filming from home or in a small studio, applying the right techniques will make a huge difference in how your audience perceives your content. In this chapter, we'll explore key filming techniques for beginners, including **maintaining eye contact with the camera, using natural light effectively**, and **recording multiple takes for flexibility**. Let's break them down:

1. Maintaining Eye Contact with the Camera

Why Eye Contact Matters

One of the most powerful techniques in video production is maintaining **eye contact with the camera**. This simple action helps build a connection with your audience and makes them feel like you're speaking directly to them. When you look into the camera lens, your viewers feel more engaged, as though they are part of the conversation.

- **Engagement**: Eye contact establishes trust and credibility. People naturally connect with individuals who appear focused and present. When you make eye contact with the camera, you create a more intimate and engaging experience for your audience.
- **Confidence**: Looking into the lens conveys confidence and makes your message come across more clearly. It shows that you are comfortable and assured in your delivery.

How to Maintain Eye Contact

- **Positioning the Camera**: Ensure that your camera is placed at **eye level**. This positioning allows you to look straight into the lens without needing to strain your neck or head. When you look directly into the camera, your gaze will be natural and comfortable.
- **Avoiding Distractions**: It's easy to get distracted by yourself on the screen, or by other elements in your environment. Resist the urge to look at your reflection or your notes too often. Your primary focus should be on maintaining a steady gaze at the camera.

- **Small Breaks**: While maintaining eye contact is important, you can occasionally glance away to collect your thoughts or avoid fatigue. Just ensure that your eye movements are subtle and not overly noticeable, so the connection doesn't feel interrupted.

Practice Tip

Try recording yourself while speaking to the camera and watch your footage back. Make sure you're looking directly into the lens most of the time. It can feel unnatural at first, but with practice, it will become second nature.

2. Using Natural Light Effectively

Why Natural Light is a Game-Changer

Natural light is one of the best tools for creating flattering, clear, and professional-looking video content. Unlike artificial lighting, natural light provides a soft, even glow that highlights your face without harsh shadows or overexposure.

- **Flattering Effect**: Natural light is gentle on your skin and minimizes harsh shadows. It gives your face a soft, even tone, which is perfect for videos where you want to look your best.
- **Cost-Effective**: Natural light is free! With no need for expensive studio lights, you can utilize the sunlight streaming through a window to illuminate your space.

How to Use Natural Light

- **Positioning Near Windows**: Place your filming setup near a window to take advantage of natural light. A well-lit room will provide even illumination for your face, avoiding the need for additional lighting. If you can, position yourself **facing the window** so that the light illuminates your face directly.
- **Timing Your Shoot**: The time of day affects the quality of natural light. **Golden hour** (the first hour after sunrise and the last hour before sunset) provides soft, warm lighting that is ideal for filming. Avoid midday sunlight, which can create harsh shadows and overexposure.
- **Diffusing Harsh Light**: If the sunlight is too intense, use a **sheer curtain or diffuser** to soften it. This helps prevent sharp contrasts and makes the light more flattering. Alternatively, you can use a reflector (even a whiteboard or piece of foil) to bounce the light and fill in shadows.

Avoiding Common Pitfalls

- **No Backlighting**: Ensure the light is coming from in front of you, not behind you. If you're filming with the window behind you, your face will become dark, and the background will be overexposed. Always keep your light source in front of you for the best effect.
- **Consistency**: Natural light can change quickly as clouds pass or the sun sets. Try to keep your filming time consistent to avoid drastic shifts in lighting. If you're filming for an extended period, use artificial lights as a

supplement.

3. Recording Multiple Takes for Flexibility

Why Multiple Takes are Important

As a beginner, it's essential to **embrace the idea of recording multiple takes.** Filming multiple versions of the same segment allows you to select the best take, ensuring your final video is polished and professional. This is especially helpful if you're feeling nervous or if you miss a key point while speaking.

- **Reducing Mistakes**: Even experienced YouTubers make mistakes! Recording multiple takes gives you the opportunity to get the wording right and avoid awkward pauses or stumbles.
- **Flexibility in Editing**: Having multiple takes allows you to choose the best moments from each and piece them together. This helps in creating a seamless, high-quality video.

How to Record Multiple Takes

- **Plan for Redos**: Don't be afraid to stop and redo parts of your video. If you feel like you didn't get your point across or you didn't like how you came across, simply restart that part and try again.
- **Take Short Breaks**: After each take, take a few seconds to reset and clear your mind. This helps you stay energized and focused, making it easier to stay consistent between takes.

- **Mark the Best Takes**: When filming multiple takes, make sure to **mark or note the best ones**. This could be as simple as taking a note on your phone or verbally indicating which take you liked the most so you don't waste time reviewing all of them later.

Editing Considerations

When you're editing your video, you'll have the flexibility to select clips that feel natural and polished. Mix and match the best sections to create the most engaging flow. Remember that editing is a tool that helps you create the best version of your content, and multiple takes are your best friend in this process.

Troubleshooting Common Problems

Even the most experienced YouTubers encounter issues while filming. Whether it's blurry footage, audio problems, or unexpected technical glitches, learning how to troubleshoot these common problems is crucial for maintaining a smooth and professional production process. In this chapter, we'll discuss how to handle **technical issues**, stay calm under pressure, and **learn from mistakes** to adjust as you go. Troubleshooting is a skill that improves with experience, but understanding these foundational strategies will help you tackle problems efficiently.

1. Dealing with Technical Issues (Blurry Footage, Audio Problems)

Blurry Footage

One of the most common technical issues beginners face is **blurry footage**. This can occur for various reasons, but the good news is that it's often easy to fix.

- **Check Your Focus**: The first thing to check is whether your camera is properly focused. Many cameras (even smartphones) have autofocus, but sometimes it doesn't function as well in low-light situations or when there's a lot of movement. To avoid this, make sure you lock the focus or manually adjust it if your camera allows it. Focus on a nearby object or yourself before recording to ensure sharp footage.
- **Lens Cleanliness**: Dust or smudges on your lens can cause blurry footage. Regularly clean your camera lens with a microfiber cloth to ensure clear shots.
- **Proper Resolution**: Ensure that you're filming in the right resolution. For YouTube, it's recommended to film in **1080p** or **4K** for the best quality. Check your camera settings before you begin filming to ensure that it's set to record at the desired resolution.

Audio Problems

Audio issues are equally frustrating, but they can often be resolved by troubleshooting a few key areas:

- **Check Your Microphone**: Whether you're using a built-in camera microphone or an external mic, make sure that it's securely connected and functioning. If you're using a

USB microphone, check the connection and ensure that the device is selected in your audio settings.
- **Test Before You Shoot**: Always test your microphone and audio levels before you start filming. Record a short test clip to check for issues like background noise, muffled sound, or audio distortion.
- **Minimize Background Noise**: Audio quality is heavily impacted by the environment you're filming in. If you're filming in a noisy area, try using soundproofing techniques, such as turning off nearby appliances or closing windows to reduce external noise. You can also use **lapel microphones** or **directional microphones** to capture clear audio while filtering out unwanted background sounds.
- **Backup Audio Solutions**: If you've recorded an entire video with poor audio, consider using a backup audio track. This can be either a voiceover or an external audio recording synced in post-production.

Fixing Video or Audio Sync Issues

Sometimes, video and audio may go out of sync during filming. This issue is most commonly seen when using external microphones or when there are delays in the recording process. If this happens:

- **Manual Syncing**: In your editing software, use markers or the visual cues (such as claps or other loud noises) to manually synchronize the audio and video tracks.
- **Export and Re-import**: If you notice persistent sync issues, export the video and re-import it into your editing

software, as this often helps resolve timing discrepancies.

2. Staying Calm Under Pressure

Managing Stress During Troubleshooting

It's easy to get frustrated when things don't go as planned, especially when you've already invested time and energy into creating content. However, staying calm and composed is key to resolving technical issues efficiently. Here's how to keep your cool:

- **Take a Breather**: If you're feeling overwhelmed, take a moment to step away. It's easy to become frustrated when you're too focused on the issue. A short break can help clear your mind and reset your problem-solving approach.
- **Identify the Problem Systematically**: Instead of panicking, take a deep breath and methodically troubleshoot. Start by identifying the most obvious causes (e.g., checking cables, settings, etc.), and work your way through the problem systematically. This approach helps you stay in control.
- **Practice Patience**: Technical problems often require patience to resolve. Take your time, and don't feel pressured to fix everything immediately. Remember, it's okay to make mistakes, and troubleshooting is part of the learning process.
- **Stay Positive**: A positive mindset helps reduce stress and fosters a productive approach to problem-solving. Keep in mind that you've already made progress by getting started, and setbacks are just learning opportunities. Remain

confident in your ability to troubleshoot and solve the issue.

Pro Tip: Write Down Solutions

As you work through troubleshooting, consider keeping a log of solutions to problems you've encountered. This log can help you recall solutions to common issues and help you move forward faster in the future.

3. Learning from Mistakes and Adjusting on the Go

Embracing Mistakes as Learning Opportunities

No matter how prepared you are, mistakes will happen. The key is to view them as **learning opportunities** rather than setbacks. Here's how to approach mistakes constructively:

- **Reflect on What Went Wrong**: After encountering a technical issue, take a few minutes to reflect on what caused it. Was it a setting mistake? Did you forget to check your equipment? Understanding the root cause will help you avoid the same issue in the future.
- **Adjust Your Workflow**: If a technical issue arises often, think about how you can adjust your workflow to prevent it. Perhaps you need to check certain settings before each shoot or invest in better equipment. Small adjustments can save you time and energy in the long run.
- **Apply What You've Learned**: Once you've identified the problem and found a solution, apply it in your next filming session. Over time, you'll begin to anticipate common

issues and handle them more efficiently.
- **Be Flexible**: Sometimes, the solution isn't always immediate, and that's okay. Flexibility is important when troubleshooting. If you can't fix a problem right away, try recording the video differently, such as adjusting your angles or re-recording portions of the video without the problem.

Using Mistakes to Improve

As you continue filming and editing videos, make sure to **track your mistakes** and use them as stepping stones to improve your process. Keep a mental or physical checklist of what's worked well and what hasn't. This continuous improvement mindset will make you more efficient over time and help you create better-quality content with each video.

Section 3: Editing Like a Pro (Even as a Beginner)

Editing is where you refine your content, add polish, and make your video stand out.

Basic Editing Principles

Editing is where the magic happens in video creation. It's where you shape your raw footage into a polished, engaging video that resonates with your audience. In this chapter, we'll walk you through some essential **editing principles** that every YouTuber should know. By mastering these basics, you can

1. Cutting Unnecessary Parts for Clarity

The first step in editing is to ensure that your video is concise and to the point. Every second of your video should serve a purpose—whether it's providing information, entertaining, or engaging your audience. This is where cutting unnecessary parts comes in.

Why Cutting is Important

When you're filming, it's easy to get caught up in the moment and say more than you need to. These extra moments can drag the video and lose your viewer's attention. Cutting out **long pauses**, **repetitive phrases**, or **off-topic tangents** is key to maintaining a **tight, focused video**.

How to Cut Effectively

1. **Review your footage**: Once you've finished filming, go through the entire video and note where you start to go off track. Pay attention to moments where you stumble on your words or repeat yourself.
2. **Use the cut tool**: In your video editing software, use the **cut or razor tool** to remove unnecessary sections. Be sure to cut out any dead space—whether that's long silences or pauses in between thoughts. This ensures the pacing of the video flows smoothly.
3. **Maintain a Natural Flow**: While cutting, make sure you

don't remove essential parts of your message. The goal is to tighten the video without making it feel abrupt. Always listen to how the cuts affect the flow. Ideally, cuts should be smooth and invisible to the viewer.
4. **Be mindful of pacing**: Cutting too much can make the video feel choppy. Ensure that the **rhythm of the video** remains steady. Sometimes, leaving a small pause or breathing room can actually help to emphasize key points or create a more relaxed viewing experience.

Pro Tip: Watch Your Video Multiple Times—After your initial cut, watch your video from start to finish to identify any lingering unnecessary moments or places where the flow could be smoother.

2. Adding Transitions and Text Overlays

Transitions and text overlays are great tools for improving the flow of your video and keeping it engaging. They can help you **move from one scene to the next** smoothly and reinforce your message visually.

Transitions

Transitions are effects that move you from one clip to another, adding variety and flow to your video. While it's tempting to use fancy transitions, it's important not to overdo it. Simple transitions are often the most effective.

1. **Types of Transitions**: The most common transitions include **cuts** (the simplest), **fades** (softens the transition

between clips), **dissolves** (gradual blending between clips), and **wipes** (one scene replacing another, often used for visual interest). Stick with **simple fades** or **cross dissolves** if you're a beginner. These transitions are professional and don't distract from the content.
2. **When to Use Transitions**: Use transitions to signify a change in scene, time, or location. For instance, if you're jumping from a discussion of one topic to the next, a fade or simple cut can signal this shift.
3. **Don't Overdo It**: Avoid using too many dramatic transitions or effects in one video, as they can become distracting and detract from the content. Keep your transitions simple and purposeful.

Text Overlays

Text overlays are a powerful way to highlight important points, provide additional context, or even add a bit of personality to your video.

1. **Adding Text for Emphasis**: You can use text overlays to emphasize key phrases or quotes. For example, if you mention a statistic or an important piece of information, adding **bold text** on screen can help reinforce the message.
2. **Using Text for Clarification**: Text overlays are also useful when introducing new concepts or when you want to ensure your audience retains specific information. You might add definitions, reminders, or steps on the screen as you talk.
3. **Style and Consistency**: Keep your text consistent in

terms of style, size, and color. Don't use too many different fonts or colors, as this can make the video feel chaotic. Stick to one or two fonts and ensure the text is easy to read against your video background.
4. **Placement**: Place text in areas that don't cover important visuals. Typically, text is placed in the **upper or lower thirds** of the screen. Ensure it doesn't obstruct the main action, whether that's your face, product shots, or a demonstration.

Pro Tip: Animations: You can animate text to make it more dynamic. Subtle animations—like having text fade in and out or slide across the screen—can make your video feel more polished without being overwhelming.

3. Syncing Audio and Video Seamlessly

One of the most important aspects of video editing is making sure that the **audio and video are perfectly synchronized**. This is especially crucial if you're recording audio separately from your video or if there's a delay in your camera or microphone.

Why Syncing Matters

If your audio and video aren't in sync, it can break the immersion for your viewers, making it uncomfortable to watch. It's important to make sure that the sound matches the visuals, so everything feels natural and cohesive.

How to Sync Audio and Video

1. **Using Visual Cues**: The most common way to sync audio and video is by using a **visual cue**, such as a loud clap at the beginning of your video or a sharp visual action like a hand movement. When you clap, the sound and motion will appear on your editing timeline. Use this cue to line up the audio track with the video footage.
2. **Check for Audio Drift**: Over time, audio and video can drift out of sync, especially if you're using multiple devices. In your editing software, zoom in on the timeline and visually match the waveform of the audio to the corresponding video. Make adjustments if necessary to keep everything in sync.
3. **Use Audio Syncing Tools**: Some editing software, like Adobe Premiere Pro and Final Cut Pro, has automatic syncing tools that will help you match your video and audio. These tools work by analyzing the audio waveform, so if you're dealing with a complex shoot, these features can save you a lot of time.

Pro Tip: Double-Check Sync at Key Moments—If your video includes moments where you're speaking or presenting, make sure to double-check that the sound is still in sync throughout the entire video, especially if you're cutting between scenes.

Tools and Tutorials

When it comes to editing your YouTube videos, the right tools and knowledge are crucial to creating high-quality content. As a beginner, you don't need to invest in expensive software or spend hours learning complex systems. In this chapter, we'll introduce you to **free and beginner-friendly editing tools**, **YouTube tutorials** that will help you master the basics, and we'll also touch on **advanced features** that you can explore as you progress in your editing journey.

1. Overview of Free and Beginner-Friendly Editing Software

As a new YouTuber, you want software that's easy to use, but also capable of helping you create polished content. Thankfully, there are several great **free editing tools** that you can use to get started without any financial investment.

Free Editing Software Options:

1. **iMovie (Mac/iOS)**

- **Overview**: iMovie is a great option for beginners, especially if you're using a Mac or iOS device. It's incredibly user-friendly and comes pre-installed on Apple devices, so you don't need to download anything extra.
- **Features**: Basic editing functions like cutting, trimming, and merging clips. It also has built-in templates for transitions, titles, and effects that can help make your video look professional.
- **Why It's Good for Beginners**: The interface is simple, and it offers just the right balance of basic features and creative flexibility to get started with YouTube video editing.

1. **Shotcut (Windows, Mac, Linux)**

- **Overview**: Shotcut is a free, open-source video editor that's available for multiple operating systems. It offers a lot of functionality for beginners without the steep learning curve of professional software.
- **Features**: Includes multi-track editing, video filters, transitions, and even audio editing capabilities. You can also work with a wide variety of file formats.
- **Why It's Good for Beginners**: It's an open-source tool, meaning it's free and regularly updated. Shotcut also has a wide range of tutorials available online to help you learn quickly.

1. **DaVinci Resolve (Windows, Mac, Linux)**

- **Overview**: DaVinci Resolve is a powerful, professional-grade video editor that's available for free. It's perfect for beginners who want to grow into more advanced editing as they gain experience.
- **Features**: DaVinci Resolve is known for its incredible color grading tools, but it also offers a complete suite of editing tools, including multi-camera editing, audio post-production, and visual effects.
- **Why It's Good for Beginners**: While it has a steeper learning curve than other tools, the free version still offers a lot of the professional features that more experienced creators use. If you're serious about growing on YouTube, this is a great option to start with.

1. **OpenShot (Windows, Mac, Linux)**

- **Overview**: OpenShot is a free, open-source video editor

that is easy to use and packed with features.
- **Features**: Offers unlimited tracks for audio and video, drag-and-drop functionality, various video effects, and 3D animation. It also has powerful keyframe animation tools, so you can get creative with your edits.
- **Why It's Good for Beginners**: OpenShot's clean and simple interface makes it easy for beginners to get started, and it's packed with powerful features to help you take your editing to the next level.

Which Software Should You Choose?

- If you're using a **Mac** or **iOS**, start with **iMovie**—it's simple, fast, and effective.
- For **Windows** users, both **Shotcut** and **OpenShot** are excellent free options.
- If you're looking for a **long-term tool** that will grow with you as your skills improve, **DaVinci Resolve** is worth exploring.

2. YouTube Tutorials for Mastering the Basics

Learning to edit takes practice, but you don't have to go it alone. There's an **abundance of free YouTube tutorials** that can guide you through the basics of video editing, teaching you everything from the simplest edits to advanced techniques. Here are a few **key tutorial channels** and **resources** for getting started:

CHAPTER 3: CREATING AND EDITING YOUR FIRST VIDEO

Beginner YouTube Editing Tutorials

1. **Justin Brown - Primal Video**

- **Channel Overview**: Justin Brown's Primal Video channel offers beginner-friendly tutorials on video editing, content creation, and YouTube growth. The tutorials focus on simplicity and getting the best results with the tools available to you.
- **What You'll Learn**: How to use basic editing tools, time-saving tips, and easy tricks to improve the quality of your videos with free or affordable software.

1. **Filmora**

- **Channel Overview**: Filmora's YouTube channel features step-by-step tutorials on using their software, which is a great option for those who prefer something easy to use. Even if you're not using Filmora, their tutorials are excellent for beginners looking to learn basic video editing principles.
- **What You'll Learn**: How to cut, trim, add text overlays, transitions, and effects—essential skills for any beginner editor.

1. **Peter McKinnon**

- **Channel Overview**: Peter McKinnon is a professional YouTuber and photographer who offers high-quality tutorials on everything related to video production, including editing, lighting, and creative effects. Although he often

uses premium software, his tips can easily be adapted to beginner software as well.
- **What You'll Learn**: How to create cinematic videos, including color grading, sound design, and creative editing techniques. His tutorials also cover the mindset and workflow behind successful video editing.

1. **Skillshare / Udemy**

- **Overview**: For those willing to invest a little more time, Skillshare and Udemy offer affordable video editing courses, often tailored specifically to YouTubers and content creators. These courses range from absolute beginner to intermediate levels.
- **What You'll Learn**: In-depth tutorials on editing software, tips on YouTube video production, and techniques for enhancing your videos.

YouTube Tutorials to Get Started

- **"How to Edit Your First YouTube Video"** by Filmora
- **"YouTube Video Editing for Beginners"** by Justin Brown
- **"Editing Basics for YouTube Videos"** by Peter McKinnon

These free resources will guide you through the technical aspects of editing and also give you creative insights that will make your videos stand out. Make sure to watch multiple tutorials for different perspectives and styles, and don't forget to practice!

3. Exploring Advanced Features as You Progress

As you become more comfortable with the basics of editing, you'll want to start experimenting with advanced features to improve the quality of your videos. Here are some editing tools and techniques you can explore once you've mastered the basics:

Advanced Editing Features to Explore:

1. **Color Grading**

- **Why It's Useful**: Color grading can transform your footage, making it look more professional and cinematic. You can adjust the brightness, contrast, saturation, and color balance to create a specific mood or feel for your videos.
- **What to Use**: DaVinci Resolve is excellent for color grading, but even tools like iMovie and Shotcut allow basic color correction.

1. **Green Screen (Chroma Keying)**

- **Why It's Useful**: If you want to place yourself in different environments or add dynamic visual effects, a green screen (also known as chroma key) is a powerful tool.
- **What to Use**: DaVinci Resolve, iMovie, and Shotcut all support green screen effects.

1. **Animation and Motion Graphics**

- **Why It's Useful**: Adding animation and motion graphics can make your videos more engaging and visually appealing. You can use this to introduce text, animate logos, or even create unique effects.
- **What to Use**: Advanced software like Adobe Premiere Pro or DaVinci Resolve offers these features, but tools like OpenShot also provide basic animation capabilities.

1. **Multi-Camera Editing**

- **Why It's Useful**: If you're shooting a scene from multiple angles or with multiple cameras, multi-camera editing allows you to switch between different video sources smoothly.
- **What to Use**: DaVinci Resolve and Adobe Premiere Pro have excellent multi-camera editing tools, but Shotcut also offers basic multi-track editing.

Pro Tip: Start small. As you progress, you can gradually incorporate advanced features into your videos. Focus on one technique at a time—whether it's color grading, animation, or green screen—so you don't get overwhelmed.

Polishing Your Video

Once you've completed filming and editing your video, the final step is to polish it before uploading it to YouTube. This process ensures your video is **error-free**, **visually appealing**, and **ready for public viewing**. In this chapter, we'll walk you through the steps for **reviewing your video for errors and flow**, **exporting it in the best quality**, and **saving backups** so your hard work is preserved and easily accessible for future use.

1. Reviewing for Errors and Flow

Even with careful planning, it's easy to overlook minor mistakes during the editing process. That's why a thorough review is essential before exporting your final video. Follow these steps to ensure your video is polished and professional:

Step 1: Watch the Entire Video

- Play the video from start to finish without interruptions.
- Take notes on any sections that feel awkward, rushed, or too slow.
- Look for errors such as:
- Misspelled text overlays or captions.
- Sudden audio drops or uneven volume levels.
- Awkward cuts or transitions.
- Background noise or distracting elements.

Step 2: Focus on Flow

- Does the video have a natural progression?
- Is the **hook** at the beginning attention-grabbing?
- Does the **middle section** deliver value without rambling or unnecessary information?
- Is the **call-to-action** at the end clear and compelling?

Step 3: Fine-Tune Edits

- Trim any parts that feel repetitive or drag on too long.
- Ensure all transitions are smooth and don't feel abrupt.
- Add final touches like background music, sound effects, or additional text overlays to emphasize key points.
- Check that any branding elements, such as logos or watermarks, are correctly positioned and visible.

Pro Tip: Watch your video on different devices (computer, phone, and tablet) to see how it looks and sounds across platforms. This step helps catch issues that may not be noticeable on your editing screen.

2. Exporting Your Video in the Best Quality

Exporting your video in the right format and resolution is crucial for maintaining high visual and audio quality when it's uploaded to YouTube. Here's a step-by-step guide to exporting your polished video:

Step 1: Choose the Right Format

- Use **MP4** format with **H.264 codec**—this is YouTube's recommended file type for high-quality videos.
- Avoid formats that may compress your video too much, as this can reduce the quality significantly.

Step 2: Optimize Resolution and Frame Rate

- For most YouTube videos, export at **1080p (Full HD)** with a **16:9 aspect ratio** and **30 frames per second (fps)**.
- If you recorded in 4K, you can export in **4K resolution (2160p)** for ultra-high-definition quality, especially if your audience watches on larger screens.
- Match the frame rate you filmed in (usually 24fps, 30fps, or 60fps) to avoid motion blur or uneven playback.

Step 3: Adjust Bitrate and Audio Settings

- **Bitrate Recommendations:**
- **1080p**: 8–12 Mbps.
- **4K**: 35–45 Mbps.
- **Audio Settings:**
- Export in **AAC** format with a **128 kbps or higher** bitrate for crisp, clear sound.

Step 4: Test Before Uploading

- Watch the exported file in its entirety to confirm that no glitches occurred during the rendering process.
- Double-check the audio synchronization, video resolution, and overall quality.

3. Saving Backups for Future Use

After exporting your video, the final step is to **save backups** to ensure your work is preserved and accessible for later revisions or repurposing. Losing files due to accidental deletion, hardware failure, or corruption can be devastating—so taking time to create backups is a must.

Step 1: Save Multiple Copies

- **Original Footage**: Keep the raw, unedited clips in a dedicated folder. These can be useful for repurposing content later.
- **Edited Project Files**: Save the project files created in your editing software. This allows you to make future edits without starting from scratch.
- **Final Exported Video**: Save the polished, exported video as your primary upload file.

Step 2: Use External Storage and Cloud Services

- **External Hard Drives**: Store a copy of your video files on an external hard drive or USB drive for safekeeping.
- **Cloud Storage**: Upload your files to **Google Drive**, **Dropbox**, or **OneDrive** for easy access and extra protection in case your local files are lost.
- **YouTube Studio Backup**: Once uploaded to YouTube, your video is stored on their servers, but having additional backups ensures you have complete control over your content.

Step 3: Organize Your Files

- Create folders by **project name** or **date** to make finding specific files easier later on.
- Include a **readme.txt file** with notes about the project,

such as video titles, keywords, or edits made, to simplify updates or future content creation.

Quick Checklist: Polishing Your Video

- **Review and Edit**: ✔ Watch for errors, pacing, and flow.
- **Export Settings**: ✔ Use MP4, 1080p or 4K, H.264 codec, and 30fps.
- **Backups Created**: ✔ Save raw footage, edited files, and final exports locally and in the cloud.

5

Chapter 4: Uploading and Sharing Your First Video

Section 1: Uploading Your Video to YouTube

Uploading your video to YouTube is an essential step in sharing your content with the world. It's more than just hitting the "upload" button; you need to ensure your video is set up to maximize its visibility, engagement, and discoverability. This section will walk you through the process step-by-step.

Step-by-Step Guide to Uploading

Uploading your video to YouTube is the moment you've been working toward—it's when your content finally becomes available to viewers around the world. In this chapter, we'll walk you through the process step-by-step, from navigating the YouTube Studio interface to choosing the right settings and deciding whether to publish immediately or schedule for later.

1. Navigating the YouTube Studio Interface

YouTube Studio is the control center for managing your channel. Here's how to get started:

Step 1: Sign In to Your Account

- Go to studio.youtube.com and log in using your Google account credentials.

Step 2: Access the Upload Feature

- Click on the "**Create**" button (camera icon with a plus sign) in the top-right corner.
- Select "**Upload Videos**" from the dropdown menu.

Step 3: Select Your Video File

- Drag and drop your video file into the upload box, or click "**Select Files**" to browse for it on your computer.
- YouTube will begin processing the video immediately while you configure the settings.

2. Selecting the Right Video Settings

Choosing the correct settings is essential for optimizing your video's visibility and impact.

Step 1: Add Basic Video Details

- **Title:** Create a compelling, keyword-rich title that grabs attention and improves search rankings.
- **Description:** Write a detailed description explaining the video's content. Include relevant keywords, timestamps, and links to related content.
- **Tags:** Add keywords related to your video's topic to help it appear in search results.

Step 2: Choose Privacy Settings

- **Public:** The video is available for everyone to watch immediately.
- **Unlisted:** Only people with the link can view the video.
- **Private:** The video is visible only to you and selected users.

Step 3: Select a Category

- Pick a category that best fits your content (e.g., Education, Entertainment, or How-to & Style). This helps YouTube recommend your video to the right audience.

Step 4: Add Video Elements

- **Thumbnail:** Upload a custom thumbnail to make your video stand out.
- **Cards and End Screens:** Add clickable links to related videos, playlists, or external websites.
- **Subtitles/Closed Captions:** Upload subtitle files to make your content accessible.

Step 5: Set Age Restrictions and Audience

- Indicate whether your video is made for kids or not, as required by COPPA regulations.
- Add an age restriction if the content isn't suitable for younger viewers.

3. Publishing vs. Scheduling Your Video

Deciding when to release your video can impact its performance. Here's how to publish or schedule effectively:

Option 1: Publish Immediately

- Once you're satisfied with your settings, click **"Publish"** to make your video live.
- Share the video link on your social media platforms, website, or email list to drive traffic quickly.

Option 2: Schedule for Later

- Click the **"Schedule"** option instead of publishing.
- Choose a specific date and time for the video to go live.
- Scheduling allows you to release videos at peak viewing times for your audience, increasing engagement.

Pro Tip: Use YouTube Analytics to determine when your audience is most active and schedule accordingly.

Option 3: Premiere Feature

- Select the **"Set as Premiere"** option to create a live viewing event.

- Viewers can watch the video as it's released and interact with you in real time via live chat.
- Premieres are great for building excitement and engagement around new uploads.

Quick Checklist for Uploading Your Video

- **Upload Process:** ✔ Use YouTube Studio to upload your file.
- **Basic Details:** ✔ Add a strong title, description, and tags.
- **Settings:** ✔ Select privacy, audience, and category options.
- **Enhancements:** ✔ Upload a thumbnail and add cards or end screens.
- **Publish or Schedule:** ✔ Decide whether to go live immediately or later.

Creating Effective Titles and Descriptions

Once the basic settings are in place, you can move on to creating the elements that will help your video stand out in search results and attract views.

1. Writing Clickable, SEO-Friendly Titles

Your video title is the first thing potential viewers will see, so it needs to grab their attention while also being SEO-friendly. Here's how to craft an effective title:

- **Keep it Concise**: Titles should be clear and to the point,

ideally between 60–70 characters.
- **Use Keywords**: Incorporate keywords that are relevant to your video and likely to be searched by your target audience. This boosts your SEO and helps your video appear in search results.
- **Create Curiosity**: Pique viewers' interest by making your title intriguing. Ask a question or present a problem that your video solves.
- **Be Honest**: Make sure your title reflects the actual content of your video. Misleading titles can hurt your credibility and decrease engagement.

Examples:

- **Bad Title**: "Video About Books"
- **Good Title**: "5 Must-Read Books to Transform Your Life | Top Picks for Personal Growth"

2. Crafting Detailed, Informative Descriptions

A great description provides viewers with more context about your video while also improving your SEO.

- **First 1-2 Sentences**: The first few sentences of your description should provide a concise summary of what the video is about. This section also appears in search results, so make it compelling.
- **Add More Details**: The remaining part of your description should provide more context, such as key points discussed in the video, links to resources, or calls to action.
- **Include Keywords Naturally**: Just like your title, your

description should contain relevant keywords. Use natural language, though—avoid keyword stuffing.

Example:

- **Bad Description**: "Books, books, books, personal growth, personal growth, self-help."
- **Good Description**: "In today's video, I share my top 5 must-read books for personal growth. These books will help you build better habits, boost your productivity, and live a more fulfilled life. Make sure to check out the links below for more info and a free reading list!"

3. Using Timestamps and Hashtags Effectively

- **Timestamps**: If your video is long or covers multiple topics, consider adding timestamps in the description. This allows viewers to easily navigate to the specific sections of the video that interest them most.
- Example: "0:00 Introduction | 1:30 Why Books Are Important | 3:45 Top 5 Books"
- **Hashtags**: Hashtags can help categorize your video and improve discoverability. Place relevant hashtags in the description or title (up to 15 hashtags) without overloading the viewer with too many. Use specific, niche hashtags for better targeting.
- Example: #PersonalGrowth #BookRecommendations #SelfHelp

Designing an Eye-Catching Thumbnail

Thumbnails are the first impression that viewers get of your video. They act as a mini-advertisement, enticing potential viewers to click and watch. In a sea of content, an eye-catching thumbnail can make all the difference in whether your video gets seen or overlooked. In this section, we will explore why thumbnails are crucial for attracting views, how you can create them with simple tools like Canva, and how to test different designs to determine what resonates with your audience.

1. The Importance of Thumbnails in Attracting Views

Imagine scrolling through YouTube and seeing dozens of video titles. How do you decide which video to click on? The answer is simple: the thumbnail.

- **First Impressions Matter:** When users browse YouTube, they are bombarded with an endless amount of content. Your thumbnail is the first thing that catches their eye. A vibrant, engaging thumbnail can make your video stand out among the competition. It serves as a visual cue about what your video is about, and it can make a viewer pause their scroll and click to watch.
- **Thumbnails Drive Click-Through Rate (CTR):** The click-through rate (CTR) is a key metric that measures how many people click on your video after seeing your thumbnail. A higher CTR means your thumbnail is doing its job well. A well-designed thumbnail, in combination with a compelling title, can significantly increase your CTR and help your video gain more views.
- **Thumbnails Tell a Story:** Thumbnails should give a glimpse of what the video will deliver. If your video is

about a cooking tutorial, your thumbnail should showcase the final dish or the cooking process in an appealing way. If it's a tutorial, featuring the subject or the result can generate curiosity. A thumbnail doesn't have to cover everything but should provide enough context to make people want to learn more.
- **Brand Recognition:** Consistent thumbnail designs are an excellent way to build your brand identity. When viewers recognize your style and layout, it becomes easier for them to spot your videos among other content. Over time, your thumbnails will become synonymous with your channel, fostering trust and recognition.

2. Using Simple Tools Like Canva to Create Stunning Thumbnails

You don't need to be a graphic design expert to create professional-looking thumbnails. With easy-to-use tools like **Canva**, you can create high-quality thumbnails that capture attention without the need for expensive software. Let's walk through the process.

- **Getting Started with Canva:** Canva is a user-friendly design tool that allows you to create a variety of graphics, including YouTube thumbnails. If you don't already have a Canva account, head over to Canva.com and create one. There is a free version that includes plenty of features, but you can opt for the Pro version if you want access to additional templates, photos, and design elements.
- **Choosing the Right Dimensions:** The recommended dimensions for YouTube thumbnails are **1280 x 720 pixels**

with a 16:9 aspect ratio. Canva has built-in templates that are optimized for YouTube thumbnails, so when you search for "YouTube thumbnail" in the search bar, you'll find templates that are pre-sized and ready to customize.
- **Selecting a Template or Starting from Scratch:** Canva offers a wide range of templates designed specifically for YouTube thumbnails. These templates are fully customizable. You can choose a pre-made design that fits your video's theme or start from scratch with a blank canvas. The beauty of Canva is that you can drag and drop elements like images, text, and icons to create a thumbnail that speaks to your audience.
- **Incorporating Eye-Catching Elements:**
- **Bold, Clear Text:** When adding text to your thumbnail, ensure it's easy to read, even at smaller sizes. Use bold fonts and limit the amount of text. Short, punchy phrases work best, such as "Quick Tips!" or "Must-Try Recipe!" Avoid cluttering your thumbnail with too many words.
- **Contrasting Colors:** Use vibrant, contrasting colors to make your thumbnail pop. Bright colors like red, yellow, and blue tend to stand out on YouTube. Consider using a dark background with bold, light-colored text or vice versa. The contrast draws the eye and makes your thumbnail more visually appealing.
- **High-Quality Images:** A high-quality image can make all the difference. Canva allows you to upload your own images, or you can use free stock images from their library. Choose images that are clear and relevant to your video. For example, if your video is about a travel destination, use an attractive, high-resolution image of the location.
- **Faces and Emotions:** Thumbnails that feature people,

especially close-up shots of their faces, tend to perform better. People are naturally drawn to human faces, and using a facial expression that matches the video's tone (e.g., excitement, curiosity, humor) can generate more clicks.
- **Saving and Uploading Your Thumbnail:** Once you've finalized your design, click on the "Download" button in Canva, and choose the format you prefer (JPG or PNG). Keep the file size under 2 MB to meet YouTube's upload requirements. After downloading your thumbnail, head over to YouTube Studio and upload the image during the video upload process.

3. Testing Different Designs to See What Works

Creating the perfect thumbnail often takes some trial and error. What works for one video might not work for another, so it's essential to test different designs and see which ones resonate with your audience. Here's how you can approach testing and optimizing your thumbnails:

- **A/B Testing (Split Testing):** A/B testing is a method where you create two variations of the same thumbnail and compare their performance. This involves changing one element—such as the text, image, or color scheme—and seeing which one leads to a higher CTR. Unfortunately, YouTube doesn't offer built-in A/B testing for thumbnails, but you can test manually by updating the thumbnail after the video is published. After a few days, check your video's CTR and decide which thumbnail version is performing better.
- **Track Metrics in YouTube Analytics:** Once you've

uploaded a thumbnail, you can monitor its performance in YouTube Analytics. Key metrics to track include:
- **CTR (Click-Through Rate):** How often people click on your video after seeing the thumbnail.
- **Watch Time and Engagement:** The number of views, average view duration, and engagement (likes, comments) can also be indicative of how well your thumbnail attracted the right audience.
- **Look at What Works for Other Creators:** Research what works for successful creators in your niche. Notice their thumbnail designs—what elements do they consistently use? What colors, fonts, and image styles are common? Studying their thumbnails will give you insight into what resonates with viewers in your content category. However, make sure to create a thumbnail that is uniquely yours. While inspiration is great, avoid copying.
- **Learn from Past Videos:** Review past videos and look for patterns. Did certain thumbnails perform better than others? If so, analyze why. Did the brighter colors perform better, or was it the type of text used? Over time, you will develop a better understanding of what works for your specific audience.

Section 2: Promoting Your First Video

Now that your video is live on YouTube, the next crucial step is to get the word out and drive traffic to your video. Simply uploading your content isn't enough; you need to actively promote it to gain visibility, engage with your audience, and grow your channel. In this section, we'll explore how to effectively promote your first video across different platforms, collaborate with other creators, and understand YouTube's analytics to improve your strategy.

Sharing on Social Media

In today's digital world, simply uploading a video to YouTube isn't enough to ensure success. To truly get your video seen and increase its chances of going viral, you need to share it across various social media platforms. Social media is a powerful tool that allows you to reach a wider audience, engage with viewers, and drive traffic to your YouTube channel. In this section, we will explore how to effectively share your video on platforms like Instagram, Facebook, and Twitter, how to encourage friends and family to share your content, and why interacting with your audience in the comments is crucial for building a loyal community.

1. Posting on Platforms Like Instagram, Facebook, and Twitter

To maximize the reach of your content, it's essential to leverage multiple social media platforms. Each platform has its own strengths and audience, and by sharing your videos strategically, you can draw in a wider range of viewers.

- **Instagram: Visual Appeal and Short Clips**

Instagram is one of the most popular platforms for visual

content, making it a great place to promote your YouTube videos. Here's how to effectively use Instagram:

- **Create Teasers or Highlights:** Instagram thrives on short, visually engaging content. Share a **teaser video** or **highlight clip** from your YouTube video. This should be 15-30 seconds long, showcasing the most exciting or intriguing part of the video. Use Instagram Stories, Reels, or the feed to post these snippets and create curiosity among your followers.
- **Use the Link in Bio:** Unlike other platforms, Instagram doesn't allow clickable links in posts, but you can place a link to your YouTube video in your **bio**. In your post, encourage followers to click the link in your bio to watch the full video. You can also use services like **Linktree** or **Lnk.bio** to provide multiple links in your bio.
- **Hashtags and Engagement:** Hashtags are a great way to get discovered on Instagram. Use a mix of broad and niche hashtags related to your video. For instance, if your video is about fitness, use hashtags like #FitnessMotivation, #WorkoutTips, and #HealthyLiving. This will help your post reach a wider audience interested in the topic. Don't forget to engage with people who comment on your posts to encourage more interaction.
- **Collaborations and Shoutouts:** Partnering with influencers or creators in your niche can significantly increase the visibility of your content. Look for opportunities to collaborate or ask influencers for shoutouts, which can drive traffic to your YouTube channel.
- **Facebook: Share in Groups and Pages**

Facebook has billions of active users and offers a variety of ways to share content effectively:

- **Post on Your Profile and Page:** Share your video link directly on your **Facebook profile** and **Facebook page** with a compelling caption. Highlight the key points of your video and add a call-to-action (CTA) encouraging your followers to watch and share. Facebook's algorithm favors engaging posts, so make sure your caption is attention-grabbing and prompts people to comment.
- **Share in Relevant Facebook Groups:** Facebook groups are communities based around common interests. Find and join groups related to the content of your video. For example, if you create travel vlogs, share your video in travel groups. Be sure to read the group rules and contribute meaningfully rather than just spamming the link.
- **Boosting Your Post:** If you want to get more eyes on your video, you can pay for Facebook ads to boost your post. Facebook allows you to target specific demographics, which means you can reach people who are likely to be interested in your content.
- **Engage with Comments:** After sharing your video, make sure to reply to any comments on your post. This creates a sense of community and encourages more people to engage with your content.
- **Twitter: Quick Updates and Direct Links**

Twitter is known for its real-time updates and fast-paced nature, so it's important to craft your post in a way that catches attention quickly.

- **Short and Snappy Tweets:** Since Twitter has a character limit, keep your message short but powerful. Use a combination of engaging text, emojis, and a direct link to your YouTube video. For example, "New video alert! Watch my latest tutorial on how to create amazing thumbnails in Canva: [link] #YouTubeTutorial #Canva #VideoCreation"
- **Hashtags and Trends:** Twitter is hashtag-driven, so use relevant hashtags to increase visibility. You can also take advantage of trending hashtags related to your niche or current events. If your video is timely or taps into popular culture, using a trending hashtag can help your tweet gain more attention.
- **Retweets and Mentions:** Encourage followers to **retweet** your post to increase its reach. You can also mention other creators or influencers in your tweet if their work is relevant to your video, which can encourage them to share your content with their followers.
- **Engagement and Interaction:** Twitter is a conversational platform, so engaging with comments and retweets is key. Respond to people who comment on your posts or retweet your content. Showing appreciation for your audience can build stronger connections and encourage more interaction.

2. Encouraging Friends and Family to Share

While posting on social media platforms can help increase your reach, don't forget the power of your personal network. Friends and family can be your first advocates, helping you spread the word and share your videos with their networks.

- **Ask for Support:**Don't hesitate to directly ask friends and family to share your video. Explain to them why you're excited about it and how sharing the content will help you grow your channel. People are often happy to support their loved ones, especially if you make it easy for them.
- **Provide Ready-to-Share Content:**Sometimes, your friends and family may not know what to say when sharing your video. Make it easy for them by giving them a short, catchy caption they can copy and paste. For example, "Check out this amazing video from [Your Name] on how to design perfect YouTube thumbnails! [Link]" This removes the guesswork and makes it more likely they will share your video.
- **Engage with Their Posts:**When your friends and family share your content, make sure to engage with their posts by liking, commenting, or sharing them as well. This shows appreciation and encourages others to do the same.

3. Engaging with Your Audience in Comments

Social media is not just about sharing your content—it's also about building relationships and engaging with your audience. The more you engage, the more likely your followers will feel connected to you and share your content with others.

- **Responding to Comments on Your Posts:**When people comment on your social media posts, make sure to take the time to respond. Whether it's a question, a compliment, or a discussion point, showing that you're active and approachable will make your audience feel valued. Engaging with comments also boosts the post's visibility

in the algorithm.
- **Creating Conversations:**Ask questions or start a discussion in the comments section. For example, if you've posted a video about a specific topic, ask your audience their opinions or experiences related to that subject. Encouraging dialogue helps to foster a sense of community and keeps your audience coming back for more.
- **Acknowledging Your Fans:**Show appreciation for your most dedicated followers. Respond to their comments, share their posts, or give them a shout-out on your own social media profiles. This will encourage more people to engage with your content, knowing they might receive recognition as well.
- **Using Polls and Interactive Content:**Platforms like Instagram Stories, Twitter, and Facebook allow you to create polls or quizzes. Use these tools to engage with your audience in a fun and interactive way. Polls about your next video topic or feedback on past videos can also give you valuable insights into what your audience wants to see.

Collaborating for Visibility

In the competitive world of YouTube, standing out can be challenging, especially when you're just starting out. One of the most effective ways to gain visibility, grow your audience, and increase your channel's reach is by **collaborating** with other creators. Collaboration opens doors to new viewers, builds relationships within your niche, and can bring fresh ideas to your content. In this section, we'll explore how to collaborate with small creators in your niche, join YouTube communities and forums, and build meaningful relationships for future collaborations that can help you grow your channel.

1. Partnering with Small Creators in Your Niche

While big-name collaborations with well-established YouTubers might seem like the dream, partnering with **small creators in your niche** can be just as beneficial—if not more so. Smaller creators are often more accessible, and collaborating with them can lead to a mutually beneficial relationship. Here's how to partner with smaller creators:

- **Find Creators with Similar Audiences:** When selecting a creator to collaborate with, look for someone who shares a similar audience to yours. They don't need to have the exact same number of subscribers, but they should create content that aligns with your niche. For example, if you make educational videos on photography, consider collaborating with someone who offers related content, like editing tutorials or gear reviews. By partnering with creators who cater to the same audience, you increase the chances that their followers will be interested in your content, too.
- **Look for Creators with Engaged Audiences:** It's not just about numbers. Sometimes, smaller creators with fewer subscribers have highly engaged communities that are loyal and active. Check their comment sections and social media for signs of strong engagement. A creator with 1,000 subscribers but a highly interactive audience can be a better collaborator than someone with 10,000

subscribers but little engagement.
- **Reach Out with a Personal Touch:** When contacting potential collaborators, avoid sending generic messages. Take the time to watch a few of their videos and leave thoughtful comments on their content. Show that you appreciate their work and explain why you think a collaboration would be beneficial for both of you. Personalizing your outreach makes your proposal more genuine and increases your chances of getting a positive response.
- **Propose Clear Ideas:** When you pitch the idea for collaboration, be clear about the type of content you'd like to create together. Whether it's a **collaborative video**, a **shoutout exchange**, or a **joint livestream**, clearly outline how you envision the collaboration working. Small creators are more likely to collaborate with you if they understand the value of the partnership and the mutual benefits involved.
- **Collaboration Ideas for Small Creators:**
- **Guest Appearances:** Appear as a guest on each other's channel, sharing insights or contributing to a project.
- **Challenge Videos:** Participate in or create challenge videos together. These are engaging, shareable, and can encourage viewers to check out both of your channels.
- **Shoutouts and Cross-Promotion:** If creating content together isn't feasible, you can simply promote each other's channels. A shoutout in a video or a shared post on social media can help increase both of your audiences.
- **Collaborative Playlists:** Create playlists with videos from both of your channels, making it easier for viewers to discover new content.

By working with smaller creators, you not only expand your reach but also build a strong network of like-minded content creators who can support each other's growth.

2. Joining YouTube Communities and Forums

Another way to boost your visibility and connect with other creators is by actively participating in **YouTube communities** and **forums**. These spaces allow you to share your content, engage with others, and receive feedback. Let's explore how to get involved in these communities:

- **YouTube Creator Communities:** YouTube itself has a built-in platform for creators to interact—YouTube Creator Community. This space allows you to ask questions, share experiences, and discover tips and resources. The more active you are in these communities, the more likely you are to connect with other creators and potential collaborators.
- **Reddit Communities:** Reddit is home to various subreddits dedicated to YouTube creators, where you can share your content, discuss strategies, and network with others in your niche. Subreddits like **r/YouTube**, **r/NewTubers**, and **r/YouTubeCreators** are great places to get started. Be mindful of the rules in each subreddit—many discourage self-promotion unless you're also actively participating in discussions and providing value to the community.
- **Pro Tip:** If you post your video, make sure it's relevant to the conversation or community you're participating in. Redditors are sensitive to spam, and your post should add value to the group.

- **Discord Communities:** Discord has become a popular platform for creators to connect in real time. Many YouTubers host their own servers or join servers related to their niche, where you can network, ask for feedback, or discuss potential collaborations. Look for servers that focus on creators, video production, or your specific niche to find like-minded individuals who are interested in collaborating.
- **Facebook Groups:** Many Facebook groups are dedicated to YouTube creators and niche communities. For example, there are groups for creators focused on travel vlogs, gaming, beauty, tech, and more. These groups often host challenges, share opportunities for collaboration, and discuss best practices. Participating in these groups can help you build relationships with creators who share your interests and goals.
- **Engaging in Comments and Content Sharing:** Engaging with other creators in these communities is essential. Respond to their posts, provide constructive feedback, and share your thoughts on their content. Be an active member, not just someone looking for self-promotion. This will help you build trust and credibility, making others more likely to want to collaborate with you.

3. Building Relationships for Future Collaborations

Collaboration is not just a one-time opportunity—it's an ongoing process of building and nurturing relationships with other creators. Here's how to lay the foundation for future collaborations:

- **Focus on Long-Term Relationships:**Instead of seeing collaborations as a one-off opportunity, approach them as a way to build long-term relationships with other creators. Stay in touch even after a collaboration ends, and continue supporting each other's work. A genuine, ongoing connection will keep the door open for future projects together.
- **Support Creators Beyond Collaborations:**Collaboration isn't always about working together on content. Sometimes, it's about showing support in other ways. Share their videos, comment on their posts, or simply encourage them in their journey. The more you show genuine support for others, the more likely they are to reciprocate and collaborate with you in the future.
- **Attend Creator Events and Meetups:**Whether virtual or in person, YouTube events and creator meetups can be great opportunities to meet fellow creators in your niche. These events allow you to network, discuss collaboration ideas, and form partnerships that can lead to future content opportunities.
- **Be Professional and Respectful:**Professionalism and respect go a long way in building strong working relationships. When collaborating, be punctual, communicate clearly, and follow through on promises. By being reliable, you'll earn a reputation as someone who is easy to work with, which makes others more likely to collaborate with you again.
- **Leverage Collaborations for Future Growth:**After a collaboration, it's important to keep the momentum going. Keep engaging with your collaborator's audience, share updates about your collaboration on social media, and

keep the communication open for potential future collaborations. The relationships you build now can lead to greater opportunities down the road, as other creators may reach out to you for future projects.

Understanding Analytics

As a YouTube creator, one of the most powerful tools at your disposal is **YouTube Analytics**. Understanding and analyzing the data behind your videos is crucial for growing your channel, refining your content strategy, and reaching a larger audience. YouTube provides detailed insights into how your videos are performing, allowing you to make data-driven decisions that can improve your content and engagement. In this section, we'll dive into the basics of YouTube Analytics, explain how to track key metrics like views, watch time, and engagement, and provide strategies for using this data to improve your future videos.

1. Introduction to YouTube Analytics

YouTube Analytics is a comprehensive tool provided by YouTube that helps creators monitor the performance of their videos. It gives you insights into how viewers interact with your content, which can help you refine your strategies and make informed decisions about what type of content to create next. To access your YouTube Analytics, simply go to YouTube Studio, where you'll find a dedicated section for Analytics.

Key Features of YouTube Analytics:

- **Overview:** This is where you can get a snapshot of your channel's performance, including metrics like total views, watch time, subscriber count, and estimated revenue (if applicable). The Overview tab shows you how well your channel is doing over time and highlights recent trends.
- **Reach Tab:** This shows how your videos are being discovered. It includes metrics like impressions (how often your video thumbnails were shown), click-through rate (CTR), and traffic sources (where viewers found your video, such as YouTube search, external websites, etc.).
- **Engagement Tab:** This is where you can find data on how long viewers are watching your videos, including average view duration and total watch time. It also provides insights into which videos are getting the most engagement.
- **Audience Tab:** This provides demographic information about your viewers, such as age, gender, location, and the times they're most likely to be watching your content. It also shows how many of your viewers are returning versus new viewers.

Why It's Important: Understanding YouTube Analytics helps you optimize your content. If a video performs well, you can replicate that success by creating more videos in a similar style, format, or topic. On the other hand, if a video doesn't perform as expected, you can analyze the data to see where things went wrong and adjust your strategy accordingly.

2. Tracking Views, Watch Time, and Engagement

Now that you understand the importance of YouTube Analytics, let's dive deeper into three of the most critical metrics: **views**, **watch time**, and **engagement**. These metrics provide a clear picture of how well your videos are resonating with your audience.

- **Views:**
- **What It Is:** Views indicate how many times your video has been watched. It's one of the most basic but important metrics, as it gives you an idea of how popular your content is. However, views alone don't tell the full story. A video with high views might still have a low engagement rate or a high drop-off rate, which signals potential issues.
- **How to Use It:** Track the number of views your videos are getting over time to see which topics or video styles are resonating most with your audience. If you notice a spike in views, try to analyze what made that video stand out—was it a trending topic, a popular keyword, or an interesting thumbnail?
- **Watch Time:**
- **What It Is:** Watch time measures the total amount of time viewers have spent watching your videos. This metric is crucial because YouTube's algorithm favors videos with higher watch time, as it suggests that people find the content engaging and relevant.
- **How to Use It:** Aim to increase your average watch time per video. You can do this by creating compelling, engaging content that keeps viewers watching. Pay attention to **Audience Retention** graphs within Analytics, which

show at what point in the video people stop watching. A sharp drop in the graph could indicate that you're losing your audience early, perhaps due to a slow intro, irrelevant content, or unclear value proposition.

Pro Tip: To improve watch time, make your intros more engaging, avoid unnecessary filler, and deliver value quickly. Engaging storytelling and keeping content concise often helps.

- **Engagement (Likes, Comments, Shares, and Subscribers):**
- **What It Is:** Engagement measures how your viewers are interacting with your video. It includes metrics like likes, comments, shares, and the number of new subscribers gained from a specific video. High engagement signals to YouTube that your content is worth recommending to others.
- **How to Use It:** High engagement rates typically suggest that your content is striking a chord with viewers. Monitor which videos are getting the most likes, comments, and shares to understand what topics or video styles resonate with your audience. If a video has a high level of engagement, take note of the type of content, the video's length, the call to action (CTA), and the overall vibe of the video.

Pro Tip: Encourage engagement by including CTAs in your videos, such as asking viewers to like, comment, share, or subscribe. Additionally, responding to comments can foster community and increase engagement, which in turn signals to YouTube that your video is valuable.

3. Using Data to Improve Future Videos

Now that you know how to track views, watch time, and engagement, let's look at how you can use this data to improve your future content and grow your channel.

- **Refine Your Content Strategy:** Analyze which videos are performing best in terms of watch time, engagement, and views. What do these videos have in common? Is it the topic, the video length, the editing style, or the time of day you posted? Once you identify patterns, you can replicate these elements in future videos. For example, if your "how-to" videos have higher watch time than your vlog-style videos, you may want to create more tutorials or instructional content.
- **Optimize Your Thumbnails and Titles:** YouTube Analytics also provides insights into **click-through rate (CTR)**, which measures the percentage of people who clicked on your video after seeing the thumbnail. If your CTR is low, you may need to improve your thumbnails and titles. A compelling thumbnail and title can significantly increase the likelihood of someone clicking on your video. Look at which thumbnails and titles are generating higher CTRs and see what you can learn from them.
- **Test Different Video Lengths:** Analytics also shows your **average view duration**, which tells you how long people are sticking around in your videos. If viewers are dropping off early, try testing shorter videos to see if they maintain interest better. Alternatively, if you notice that viewers tend to watch longer videos through to the end, it could mean that they enjoy more in-depth content. Use this

information to adjust your content length accordingly.
- **Focus on Audience Retention:** Pay close attention to the **Audience Retention** graphs in your Analytics. These graphs tell you where viewers drop off in your videos, helping you pinpoint potential issues. If you see a high drop-off rate in the first few seconds, it could indicate that your intro isn't engaging enough. If the drop-off happens toward the middle, it might mean that the content loses relevance or gets repetitive. Use this information to adjust the pacing and structure of your future videos to keep viewers engaged.
- **Experiment and Iterate:** Don't be afraid to experiment with different content types, formats, and posting times. YouTube Analytics provides data on which videos are getting the most views during certain days or hours. Test different posting schedules to see when your audience is most active. Likewise, experiment with different video formats—perhaps trying out vlogs, tutorials, interviews, or reaction videos—and track how each performs.
- **Track Audience Demographics and Interests:** The **Audience** tab in Analytics shows demographic information about your viewers, such as their age, gender, location, and interests. Use this data to tailor your content to better serve your target audience. If you see that a significant portion of your audience is based in a certain country, you might create content that speaks to their culture or local interests. If your audience is predominantly young adults, you may want to adapt your style or topics to match their interests.

Section 3: Celebrating and Planning Ahead

Congratulations on uploading your first video! Whether it's a simple tutorial, a product review, or an introduction to your channel, you've just taken the first big step in your YouTube journey. But this is just the beginning. As you reflect on your journey, it's important to celebrate your progress, build momentum, and plan for the future. In this section, we'll explore how to stay motivated, keep improving, and continue creating engaging content for your audience.

Reflecting on Your Journey

As a YouTube creator, it's easy to get caught up in the rush of creating new content, analyzing performance data, and pushing for the next big milestone. However, it's equally important to take a step back and **reflect on your journey**. Reflecting not only helps you appreciate how far you've come but also provides an opportunity to acknowledge areas for growth and set meaningful goals for your future videos. In this section, we'll discuss how to celebrate the milestone of your first upload, acknowledge the areas where you can improve, and set actionable goals for your next video.

1. Celebrating the Milestone of Your First Upload

The first upload is a monumental moment in any creator's journey. It's the culmination of planning, preparing, and finally taking the leap into the world of YouTube. Whether your first video was an overwhelming success or a modest start, it's important to **celebrate** this achievement, as it marks the beginning of your creative path.

- **Acknowledge the Courage It Took to Start:** Uploading your first video requires a great deal of courage. You may have had doubts, fears, or worries about how your content would be received, but you pushed through and posted it. Take a moment to celebrate the bravery it took to get to this point. Remember, every successful YouTuber started with that same first upload.
- **Recognize the Effort You Put In:** Reflect on the time and effort you invested in creating your first video. Whether it was filming, editing, or learning how to optimize your video for YouTube, acknowledge the work you did. Starting a YouTube channel isn't easy, and the fact that you completed and published a video is an accomplishment in itself.
- **Celebrate the Small Wins:** No matter how big or small your first video's success is, celebrate it. Did you get your first view, your first like, or a comment from someone you didn't know? These small wins are steps toward building your channel. Every view and engagement is a sign that your content is being seen and appreciated, which means you're on the right path.
- **Share Your Accomplishment with Your Support System:** Celebrate your first upload with friends, family, or fellow creators who have supported you. Share the link to your video, discuss what you've learned, and bask in the pride of having taken the first step. Surrounding yourself with supportive people who celebrate your milestones will motivate you to continue creating and pushing forward.

2. Acknowledging Areas for Growth

After celebrating your first upload, it's essential to look at areas where you can **improve and grow**. Reflecting on your content and process will help you identify what worked well and what could be enhanced in future videos. Growth is an ongoing process, and every creator has areas they can improve upon.

- **Review Your Content Critically:** Take a step back and watch your first video with a critical eye. What do you like about it? What would you change if you could go back? Don't be too hard on yourself—every creator's first video is a learning experience. Look for patterns or mistakes that you can correct in future videos, whether it's in the pacing, editing, or delivery. For example, did you feel like your video had a strong hook in the first few seconds, or did you lose the viewer's attention? Did your audio come through clearly, or was it a little too quiet?
- **Consider Feedback from Viewers:** Pay attention to the feedback you've received in the comments section of your video. What are people saying? Are there any constructive suggestions or questions that could help guide your next video? Feedback from viewers—especially those who have subscribed or returned to your channel—can provide valuable insight into what your audience is enjoying or looking for.
- **Identify Skills You Want to Improve:** There are many aspects of creating YouTube videos that require ongoing improvement. You might want to work on your **video editing skills**, improve your **on-camera presence**, or get better at **SEO optimization** (title, tags, description).

Reflecting on the skills you'd like to develop can help you stay focused on your personal growth as a content creator.
- **Set Realistic Expectations for Yourself:** Growth doesn't happen overnight. It's important to set realistic expectations and acknowledge that mistakes and missteps are part of the learning process. Understand that every video you make is a step closer to honing your craft. It's normal to feel like you're not where you want to be yet, but the key is to keep improving with each upload.

3. Setting Goals for Your Next Video

Now that you've celebrated your success and acknowledged areas for growth, it's time to **set goals** for your next video. Setting goals helps you stay focused, motivated, and organized. Clear, measurable goals also give you something to strive for as you move forward in your YouTube journey.

- **Set Specific and Achievable Goals:** When setting goals, it's important that they're specific and measurable. For example, instead of saying, "I want to make a better video," try setting a goal like, "I want to increase my video's average watch time by 20% by improving the pacing and structure." Or, you could set a goal to **improve your thumbnail design** and see if it leads to higher click-through rates (CTR). Specific goals allow you to track progress and measure your success.
- **Focus on One Area of Improvement at a Time:** Don't overwhelm yourself by trying to tackle everything at once. If you've identified areas for growth (like improving your video quality, editing, or SEO), set a goal to focus on one

of them for your next video. For instance, if you want to improve your video's SEO, make it a goal to research and implement better keywords, tags, and descriptions. This will help you improve in a focused way without feeling overwhelmed by the entire process.

- **Set a Production Goal:** You might also set goals related to **your production process**. How can you streamline your workflow to create videos more efficiently? Perhaps you can commit to filming and editing your next video in a shorter time frame or trying a new editing software that will enhance your video's production value.
- **Set Engagement Goals:** Besides focusing on the production side of your videos, consider setting goals related to **audience engagement**. For example, you could set a goal to respond to every comment within 24 hours, or encourage viewers to share your video on social media. By focusing on engagement, you build a stronger connection with your audience and increase the chances of growing your community.
- **Evaluate Your Goals After Each Video:** After your next upload, reflect on how you did. Did you meet the goals you set? What went well, and what could have been improved? By evaluating your progress after each video, you can refine your goal-setting process and keep making steady progress toward your larger objectives.

Building Momentum

Building momentum on YouTube is about more than just uploading videos regularly; it's about creating a **sustained**

presence that resonates with your audience. Consistency, engagement, and long-term planning all play critical roles in ensuring your growth on the platform. Once you've gotten started, the real challenge is maintaining and building on the momentum you've created. In this section, we'll explore how to stay consistent with your content schedule, engage with your growing audience, and plan for long-term growth and success.

1. Consistency Is Key: Sticking to Your Schedule

Consistency is one of the most important factors in growing your YouTube channel. Regular uploads help build a **loyal audience** and establish your presence on the platform. But consistency doesn't just mean uploading frequently; it also means uploading with intention and structure.

- **Create a Realistic Upload Schedule:** One of the first steps to building momentum is setting a consistent upload schedule. Whether it's once a week, bi-weekly, or even once a month, it's important to choose a schedule that is **realistic** for your lifestyle. Consistency doesn't mean you have to upload every day or week if that's not feasible. What matters is that you pick a schedule that works for you and stick to it. Creating a **content calendar** can help you stay organized, plan ahead, and keep your content flowing regularly.
- **Why Consistency Matters:** YouTube rewards consistent creators. When you upload regularly, your videos are more likely to be suggested by the algorithm, and your audience will start to expect and look forward to your content.

Regular uploads keep you top of mind for your viewers, ensuring that you maintain their attention and grow your community. Plus, when you upload consistently, it allows you to **improve your skills** over time—whether in editing, presenting, or understanding what resonates with your audience.
- **Batching Content to Stay Consistent:** If your schedule is tight, consider batching your content. Filming multiple videos in one sitting and scheduling them for release over the following weeks can save you time and reduce the stress of constantly having to create new content. Batching allows you to keep your content pipeline full and ensures you meet your deadlines without compromising on quality.
- **Stick to Your Commitment:** The key to success on YouTube is following through with your commitments. If you promise your audience a certain upload schedule, do your best to stick to it. Inconsistent uploads can confuse your audience and make them less likely to come back. Let your audience know if you need to take a break or adjust your schedule, but **communication is key**—keeping your viewers in the loop helps build trust and loyalty.

2. Engaging with Your Growing Audience

As your channel grows, one of the most important things you can do is **engage with your audience**. Building an engaged community is the foundation of long-term success on YouTube. Engaging with viewers doesn't just mean replying to comments; it's about creating a two-way relationship with your audience, fostering a sense of community, and making them feel like part of your journey.

- **Respond to Comments:** Engaging with viewers through the comments section is one of the simplest but most effective ways to build a relationship with your audience. Respond to as many comments as you can—especially early on in your channel's growth. People appreciate when creators acknowledge them, and it can lead to more interaction and even word-of-mouth promotion. Responding to comments also helps to foster a sense of community and shows your audience that you care about their input.
- **Create Interactive Content:** To further engage with your audience, consider creating interactive content. This could include **Q&A sessions**, polls, or asking viewers to share their opinions in the comments. You can even ask your audience for feedback on what type of content they'd like to see next. This type of interaction not only boosts engagement but also gives you valuable insight into what your viewers enjoy or want more of.
- **Host Live Streams and Community Posts:** Live streaming on YouTube is another great way to engage with your audience in real-time. It allows for direct interaction and builds a stronger bond with your community. In addition, YouTube's **Community Tab** is a powerful tool that enables creators to post updates, polls, images, and short messages. This can be a great way to stay connected with your audience between video uploads.
- **Appreciate Your Supporters:** As your audience grows, take the time to acknowledge your loyal supporters. Whether it's by thanking regular commenters, mentioning

fans by name in videos, or running **giveaways** or **shout-out contests**, showing your appreciation fosters a stronger connection with your audience. These acts of gratitude can also help generate positive word-of-mouth promotion, which is vital for growth.

- **Personalize Your Interaction:** Personalizing your engagement goes beyond responding to comments or liking posts. Consider addressing your audience in a way that shows you know them. Use their names or reference something specific they've said. Engaging on a personal level creates a deeper connection, and your audience will appreciate that they are not just another number to you.

3. Planning for Long-Term Growth and Success

While consistency and engagement are vital for building momentum in the short term, it's equally important to think about **long-term growth**. Planning ahead and having a strategic approach will help you sustain momentum and continue growing your channel over time. This involves setting big-picture goals, diversifying your content, and continuously adapting to changes in the YouTube landscape.

- **Set Long-Term Goals:** As your channel grows, start setting **long-term goals**. These could include targets like reaching a certain subscriber count, expanding your content to different formats (e.g., from tutorials to vlogs), or monetizing your channel. Setting long-term goals will help you stay motivated, focused, and on track as you navigate the challenges of growing a YouTube channel.

For example, you could set a goal like: "In 6 months, I want to increase my average views per video by 30%" or "In 1 year, I want to hit 10,000 subscribers." These types of goals give you something to work toward, and breaking them down into smaller, actionable steps makes them feel more achievable.

- **Diversify Your Content Strategy:** Don't be afraid to try new formats or topics to keep your content fresh and attract a wider audience. Diversifying your content strategy allows you to experiment and find new opportunities for growth. You might want to explore **collaborations with other creators**, create **series** or **themed content**, or venture into different genres (e.g., from beauty tutorials to travel vlogs). Offering a variety of content keeps your audience engaged and increases your chances of reaching different segments of the YouTube audience.
- **Optimize for Search and Discoverability:** Plan to regularly optimize your video titles, descriptions, and tags for search. YouTube is a search engine, and getting discovered is crucial for growth. Research keywords in your niche and incorporate them into your metadata. As you build your catalog of videos, an optimized library will make it easier for new viewers to discover your content.
- **Adapt to YouTube's Changes:** YouTube is constantly evolving, with algorithm updates, changes to monetization policies, and shifting trends. As a creator, it's important to stay informed about these changes and adapt accordingly. Subscribe to YouTube's Creator Academy, follow YouTube news, and stay active in creator communities to keep up with any updates. Understanding these shifts and adjusting your approach will help you stay ahead of the

curve.
- **Monitor Your Progress and Adjust Your Strategy:** Regularly check your **YouTube Analytics** to see how your channel is growing. Use the insights from your analytics to adjust your content strategy, improve your videos, and stay on track to meet your long-term goals. Growth on YouTube takes time, and what works today may not work in a few months. Constantly learning and iterating is key to maintaining momentum.

Staying Motivated

The journey of becoming a successful YouTuber is filled with highs and lows. There are moments of excitement when your views spike, and there are moments of frustration when progress seems slow. Staying motivated during these ups and downs is essential to long-term success. **Motivation** is the fuel that drives consistency, creativity, and growth. But where does motivation come from, and how can you maintain it when faced with challenges? In this section, we'll explore how learning from the stories of successful YouTubers, staying adaptable, and keeping your passion alive can help you stay motivated and committed to your YouTube journey.

1. Learning from Successful YouTubers' Stories

One of the most powerful ways to stay motivated is by **learning from those who have already succeeded**. Successful YouTubers often share their journeys—both the struggles and triumphs. These stories can offer you valuable insights, provide reassurance, and inspire you when times get tough.

- **Everyone Starts Somewhere:** It's easy to compare yourself to established creators who seem to have it all figured out, but remember, **every YouTuber started from zero**. Take some time to research the early years of YouTube stars like **MrBeast**, **Emma Chamberlain**, or **PewDiePie**. They didn't achieve massive success overnight. They spent years creating content, refining their style, and learning from their mistakes. Their stories often include **failures**, **setbacks**, and moments of self-doubt. Seeing that they didn't give up despite these challenges can help you remember that success isn't a straight path.
- **Celebrate Small Wins:** When you see successful creators achieving milestones, it's easy to feel like you're not doing enough. But remember that their journeys were built on **small, incremental successes**. One viral video doesn't create a channel overnight. Successful YouTubers often celebrate the process and look at their growth as a collection of small wins. Reflect on your own journey and celebrate your progress, no matter how small. Whether it's getting your first comment, your first subscriber, or even learning a new editing trick—these are all stepping stones toward larger success.
- **Resilience in the Face of Challenges:** Many successful YouTubers have faced enormous challenges along the way, from dealing with **algorithm changes** to **negative feedback** and even **burnout**. Learning about these challenges—and how creators navigated through them—can teach you valuable lessons about **resilience**. For

example, creators like **Casey Neistat** took risks with their content and explored new creative avenues when faced with challenges, which ultimately helped them grow. Resilience in the face of obstacles is one of the most important traits of successful creators.
- **Find Inspiration in Their Growth:** Seeing how other creators have grown from humble beginnings can spark new ideas for your own channel. Take note of how they **adapted their content** or **embraced new trends**. Did they collaborate with others to expand their reach? Did they try something outside their usual niche that brought fresh excitement to their channel? These stories can inspire you to try new things, take creative risks, and think outside the box.

2. Staying Adaptable and Open to Change

The YouTube landscape is always changing. Algorithms evolve, audience interests shift, and new trends emerge. **Staying adaptable** is key to ensuring that you don't become discouraged or stagnant in your journey. Embrace change and be willing to adapt your approach.

- **Embrace YouTube's Evolving Algorithm:** One of the most important things to understand as a creator is that **YouTube's algorithm is constantly changing**. While it can be frustrating to keep up with every update, the key is to be open to these changes and view them as opportunities to learn and improve. For example, if YouTube shifts its algorithm to favor shorter videos (like YouTube Shorts), creators who are willing to embrace these changes can thrive. Staying adaptable means being willing to **test new formats, experiment with different content styles**, and **adjust your strategy** based on feedback from the algorithm.

- **Adapt to Audience Preferences:** Your audience will also evolve over time. What they liked six months ago may not be what they enjoy today. **Paying attention to their feedback**, analyzing your video analytics, and **staying in tune with trends** will help you adapt your content to keep your audience engaged. For example, if your viewers are commenting that they want more in-depth tutorials or Q&A sessions, it's a sign that you should pivot or introduce those elements into your content. Don't be afraid to **shift gears** and experiment with new ideas that excite both you and your audience.
- **Experiment with New Content and Formats:** If you find yourself feeling stuck or uninspired, try **diversifying your content.** You might feel like you've found your niche, but branching out can bring new energy to your channel. Whether it's trying a new type of video (vlogs, tutorials, challenges, etc.) or exploring a **new editing style**, adapting to new content ideas keeps you motivated and prevents burnout. Change is a natural part of growing, so don't shy away from it. If something new excites you, give it a try and see how it resonates with your audience.
- **Learn from Failures:** YouTube is not always smooth sailing. Sometimes videos won't perform as expected, or ideas won't resonate with your audience. But instead of getting discouraged, use these setbacks as opportunities to learn and adapt. Understanding what didn't work allows you to make adjustments for future videos and become a

more well-rounded creator.

3. Keeping Your Passion Alive

Passion is the driving force behind creativity. Without it, your content might start to feel flat, and you might lose the drive to keep uploading. To stay motivated, it's essential to keep your **passion alive**—especially during difficult times when you feel like giving up.

- **Remember Why You Started:** In the midst of challenges, it's easy to forget why you started your YouTube channel in the first place. Whether it was to share a passion, educate others, or simply have fun, **reconnect with your initial motivation**. Watch your first video again and remember the excitement and energy you had when you uploaded it. Revisiting your **original vision** helps reignite the passion that led you to create in the first place.
- **Create Content You Love:** It's important to **stay true to yourself** and create content that excites and inspires you. If you're only making videos for views or to chase trends, your content may start to feel disconnected from your true passions. By focusing on what you genuinely love and enjoy, you'll stay more motivated, and your passion will shine through in your videos. The best content comes from creators who are excited about what they're creating.
- **Take Breaks When Needed:** Passion can sometimes fade if you're pushing yourself too hard. If you're feeling drained, taking a **break** can help you recharge and return to your content with fresh ideas and renewed energy. Don't feel guilty about taking time off—it's essential for

avoiding burnout and staying motivated in the long run. When you come back, you'll likely find that your passion has been reignited.
- **Set Personal Challenges and Goals:** Set creative challenges for yourself to keep your content exciting. This could be something like **filming a video in a completely new format**, experimenting with a **new editing technique**, or challenging yourself to **collaborate with other creators**. Personal challenges help you stretch your abilities and make the creative process more exciting, which can help keep your motivation high.
- **Celebrate Your Journey, Not Just the Destination:** As you work toward milestones, it's easy to get fixated on the end goal. But take time to celebrate the journey. Recognize how much you've learned and how much you've grown since you started. Celebrate the small wins, like reaching 100 subscribers or mastering a new skill. Enjoying the process itself makes the journey more fulfilling, and your passion will stay alive as long as you remain focused on the joy of creation.

6

Recap and Final Thoughts

Recap of the Main Points

Congratulations, you've made it through the key steps to successfully start your YouTube journey! Let's quickly recap the main points we've covered so far:

1. **Understanding YouTube and Setting Your Goals**: We explored the power of YouTube as a platform, its global reach, and how it provides endless opportunities for personal and professional growth. We also debunked common myths about starting a channel and emphasized that you don't need expensive equipment or expert status to succeed.
2. **Defining Your Purpose and Audience**: Setting clear personal and professional goals is essential for channel success. We also discussed the importance of identifying your niche and understanding your target audience so

you can create content that truly resonates.
3. **Building a Success-Oriented Mindset**: Overcoming self-doubt, managing your time effectively, and building confidence in front of the camera were critical focus areas. These are all steps that will help you stay motivated and focused as you build your channel.
4. **Preparing for Your YouTube Journey**: From setting up your channel to planning your content strategy, we covered the essentials of designing your YouTube presence. We also discussed how to prepare your equipment and tools, setting you up for success even on a budget.
5. **Creating and Editing Your First Video**: We walked through how to structure and write your script, shoot your video, and edit like a pro—even as a beginner. These skills will help you produce quality content that's ready to impress your audience.
6. **Uploading, Promoting, and Celebrating Your First Video**: Finally, we covered the practical side of uploading, promoting, and celebrating your first video. From writing effective titles to creating eye-catching thumbnails, and learning how to promote your content, you're now equipped to share your message with the world.

Final Thoughts and Words of Encouragement

Starting a YouTube channel can be intimidating at first, but remember, every successful YouTuber started exactly where you are now—at the beginning. It takes time, consistency, and a lot of learning, but with the right mindset and tools, you'll grow and improve with each video you create. Keep going, celebrate every small victory, and embrace the process of learning and adapting as you go.

The most important thing is to keep creating content that excites you, because that passion is what will connect with your audience. Your journey on YouTube is just beginning, and with the foundation you've built, you are well on your way to success.

7

Ask for a Review

If you've found this guide helpful, I'd love to hear from you! Please consider leaving a review and sharing your thoughts on what you've learned. Your feedback will not only help me improve but also help others who are just starting their YouTube journey. Thank you for being part of this experience, and I can't wait to see the amazing content you create!

www.ingramcontent.com/pod-product-compliance
Lightning Source LLC
Chambersburg PA
CBHW052149220526
45471CB00004B/1600